FORTY GREAT MEN AND WOMEN IN ISLAM

Nur Ahmed

Adam Publishers & Distributors

Shandar Market, Chitli Qabar, Delhi-110006
Phone : 3271690

ISBN : 81-7435-026-8

© Publisher 1994
Revised Edition 1994
Price Rs. 80/-

Laser Typesetting by:-
DM Computer Designer & Composer,
Shinghal Building, Sadar Bazar,
Delhi Cantt-110010, Tel. : 3293825

Printed in India
Published by : S. Sajid Ali for
ADAM PUBLISHERS & DISTRIBUTORS
Shandar Market, Chitli Qabar, Delhi - 110006
Tel. : 3271690, 8953953

Printed at : Shah Offset Printer
Rodgran, Lal Kuan, Delhi-110006 Ph.: 7522725

CONTENTS

PREFACE

The works and achievements and services of most of the great sons and daughters of Islam are generally very little known to the world, especially to the present young Muslim generation. It will be of great value to the world at large, especially to the present Muslim world if the glimpses and special virtues of the great men and women in Islam, who by their great selfless services and devotion to duties and by their life examples and conduct and by their exemplary characters have done unprecedented services to Islam and to the humanity at large are presented in a book form. In the life examples of these great Muslims is exhibited in practice the ideals of Islam and its fundamental socialism and its broad enlightenment and tolerance and their lives and characters will best serve as inspiring examples and act as a great incentive and beacon light to the future generation, specially of the Muslim young men and students.

This book contains life sketches and distinguishing characteristics of 40 great men and women in Islam and includes that of great rulers, statesmen, religious devotees, Mujahids, freedom fighters, reformers, great national heroes etc., and is specially designed and aimed at to fulfil that noble purpose.

This book does not narrate the detailed life sketches of these great men and women, whose life sketches, outstanding characteristics are briefly recorded in this book.

The main and sole purpose in writing these life sketches of some forty great men and women is to focus and concentrate the attention of the readers, specially of our young men on the flash light and shining spots of these individual characters, so that they may inspire them with a new spirit with a new life purpose and grim determination to follow their footsteps and to serve their fellowmen and the humanity, to make the world a heaven of peace and happiness, amity and concord and fellow-feeling—of one universal human brotherhood.

NUR AHMAD
Chittagong, Bangladesh

FORTY GREAT MEN AND WOMEN IN ISLAM

I

IBN KHALDUN

The Great Philosopher of History in Islam

1. Though the histories were written mainly by the Muslim historians during the last fourteen centuries and these histories are full of wealth of rich, valuable and important informations for the students, the scholars and the research workers on the art and science of history, the Muslim historians have recorded the history of these times with great exactitude and vivid description. It was Ibn Khaldun, who first of all invented the science of history and made a beginning to develop history into an advanced art and science.

2. Ibn Khaldun (1332-1406 A. C.), the talented Muslim philosopher of history and the greatest intellect of his age, is one of the most outstanding thinkers the world has ever produced. Being the founder of science of sociology, Ibn Khaldun had the unique distinction of treating history as a science by supporting his facts with reasoning.

3. "There is nothing in the Christian Literature of the middle ages" says a famous Western critic, "worthy of being compared with it (Ibn Khaldun's history) and no Christian wrote a version with such clearness and precision on any Muslim State."

4.   Born in Tunis (North Africa) Ibn Khaldun had a chequered career during his early life, taking active part in the intriguing power politics of the small North African principalities, enjoying alternately the favour as well as disfavour of the ruler and at times taking refuge in distant Granada, the centre of Muslim culture, learning and power.

5.   His revolutionery spirit, being fed up with dirty politics of those times, was obliged to take a short respite in the suburbs of Tunis where he completed his immortal work, Al-Moqaddama or Prolegomena in 1377 A. C. Thereafter he shifted to Tunis to finish his one masterly work "Kitab-Al-Ibar" (World History), where he could get advantage of the reference books stocked in the Imperial Library of Tunis.

6.   Ibn Khaldun has acquired an undying name and fame and has won an outstanding place among the galaxy of the historical philosopher of the world. He is distinguished from the rest of the historians, because he treated history as a science and not merely as a narrative of certain events.

7.   Ibn Khaldun wrote history in the light of his new method of explanation and reasoning and developed it as a social philosophy. Explaining the art of writing history, Ibn Khaldun says in his Prolegomena: "It is only by an attentive examination and well-sustained application that we can discover the truth and guard ourselves against errors and mistakes. In fact, if we were merely to satisfy ourselves by reproducing the records transmitted by traditions, without consulting the rules furnished by experience, the fundamental principles of the art of government, of nature, even of the particular civilization, or the circumstances which characterise human society; if we are not to judge the wants which occurred in the distant times by those which are occurring under our eyes; and if we are not to compare the past with the present; we can hardly escape from falling into errors and losing the way of truth."

8.   He being the origintor of sociology, philosophical history and political economy, his works possess a striking originality recording a new system in understanding and explaining the social phenomena criticising and analysing history.

9. Ibn Khaldun has divided his historical works into three parts. The first part which is known as "Al-Moqaddama" or the famous "Prolegomena" deal with society and its origin, sovereignty, origins of towns and villages, trades, means of livelihood and sciences. This is the best part of the book in which Ibn Khaldun displays the heights of his creative gunius, in reviewing the diverse subjects such as political economy, sociology and history with a striking originality and brilliance.

10. Ibn Khaldun has viewed the origin of towns and villages from a social point of view: unlike Farabi whose views about the origin of towns and villages are theoretical only.

11. The third chapter of Ibn Khaldun's book deals with the state and the sovereignty in which Ibn Khaldun has propounded his advanced political theories that were later incorporated in the works of such celebrated thinkers as Machiavelli and Vico. Machiavelli's famous book "Prince" bears a close resemblance to the "Prolegomena" of Ibn Khaldun.

12. "At any rate" says a famous Western professor. "The priority must rightly be attributed to the Arab sociologist (Ibn Khaldun) as regards those counsels which Machiavelli, a century later gave to the ruler in his Prince.

13. The third part of Ibn Khaldun's great historical work "Kitabal-Ibar" which consists of two volumes, namely the sixth and seventh, elaborately deals with the history of Berbers and other neighbouring tribes and it also contains Ibn Khaldun's autobiography and known as "Al-Taarif".

14. Ibn Khaldun was the first to write a systematic autobiography. Before the autobiographies written by others are clumsy and dirty documents. Ibn Khaldun's autobiography bears an air of frankness.

15. Ibn Khaldun is undoubtedly the first writer who tried to explain fully the evolution and progress of society, as being caused by certain causes and factors and to explain the characteristics of race, climate, the means of production etc. and their effects on the formations of men's mind, sentiment as well as the formation of the

society. In the march of civilization he perceives an organised internal harmony.

16. Ibn Khaldun may be considered the discoverer as he himself claimed, of the true scope and nature of history. Ibn Khaldun may also be considered the real founder of the science of sociology. No writer, European or Eastern, had ever taken a view of history at once so comprehensive and philosophic.

17. Ibn Khaldun was the greatest historical philosopher Islam produced and he is the greatest of all all times. Not only is he the greatest historian of the middle ages, towering like a giant over pigmies, but one of the first philosopher of history, a forerunner of Machiavelli, Badin Velo, comte and Cournet.

18. History has always been considered as the most important subject in the educational curriculum of Muslims. The thorough knowledge of history was essential for princes, ministers and scholars alike. No education was to be complete without a detailed background of history. Even the soldiers were taught the history of the rise and fall of different nations, specially those of the Muslims. Ibn Khaldun may be called the father and founder of modern science of history.

19. It is an admitted fact that the greatest development of historiography and its elevation to the status of science owes much to the genius of Muslims. The Muslim historiography has at all times been united by the closest ties with the general development of scholarship in Islam, and the position of historical knowledge in Muslim edcuation has exercised a decisive influence upon the intellectual level of historical writing and Ibn Khaldun has done much in this direction.

II

UMAR BIN ABDUL AZIZ (717-20 A.C.)

1.   The caliphate of the Ommayid dynasty only lasted 91 years. Among the caliphs of this dynasty when the old, austere, simple, pristine, and stern Islam with its followers disciplined and noble lives, regulated relationship between man and man and its universal brotherhood and equality and liberty was tossing in the surging waves of the Ommayid heathinism, there appeared a great outstanding caliph among the Ommayid caliphs who is known in history as Umar Bin Abdual Aziz. His empire extended from the Atlantic to the high lands of Pamir.

SKETCH OF EARLY LIFE AND CAREER

2.   Umar Bin Abdul Aziz surnamed as Califa Saleh. The pious Caliph was the son of Abdul Aziz, Governor of Egypt and his mother Umme Aasim was the grand daughter of Hazart Umar Farukh, the second Caliph of Islam. He was born in 63 A. H. in Helwan, a village in Egypt. He received his early education at Medina under the fostering care of Abdulllah Bin Umar, his mother's uncle. At that time Medina was a great centre of learning and culture in the Muslim world.

3.   Young Umar was brought up by Abdullah, son of Umar second Caliph. Saleh Bin Kaison, his teacher was a men of highest learning and scholarship and of great piety and a great advocate of Islamic democracy. He did not believe in hereditary kingship and believed that office of the kingship could not be inherited but a ruler must be elected. His mother taught him the great traditions of her grand father, Hazrat Umar, the Caliph. So young Umar grew up in the most healthy and pious atmosphere.

4.   But young Umar, though a great scholar and well versed

in the Holy Quran and traditions lived a most luxurious life, best dressed and best fed; and when he was appointed the governor of Medina in 706 A. C. by Caliph Walid, his bag and baggages, were carried by 100 camels to Medina. But all these pomps and luxuries all on a sudden disappeared from him. His biographer Ibnal Jauzi has written that Umar Bin Abdul Aziz's clothes was with so many patches and he so freely mined with his fellow subjects that a stranger could not recognise him from among the common folks. He believed in the theory that a ruler must be elected by his people and should not be nominated.

5. In 704 A.C. he was called by his uncle Caliph Abdul Malek who gave in marriage his daughter Fatima to him. In 706 A.C. he was appointed the Governor of Medina by Caliph Walid.

UMAR'S WORKS AS A GOVERNOR

6. The first act of Umar on his arrival at Medina was to appoint a council of the ten eminent jurists and nobles of the city to advise him and he carried the administration of Medina always with their advice. During his two years' governorship he repaired the damage to the holy city caused by Caliph Yazid and Abdul Malek, and enlarged the mosque of the Prophet and beautified Medina with new buildings, gardens, aqueducts and improved road connecting the cities of Hejaz with the capital.

Moderate, yet firm, anxious to promote the welfare of the people whom he governed, Umar's governorship proved beneficent to all classes.

UMAR AS A CALIPH

7. In 99 Hijira, at the age of 36, Umar was nominated Caliph by the Ommayid Caliph Soleman Bin Abdul Aziz as his successor and he accepted it with great reluctance.

After Soleman's death when he became a Caliph the world saw aghast and amazed a wonderful revolution in Umar's life.

8. Umar the Caliph now realised the evil effect of policy of luxurious living, autocracy, overtaxation, personal gain and costly and corrupt administration, wholly un-Islamic in character and concept.

As soon as he became a Caliph, he rushed to the people and addressing them he said, "O, people, I have been nominated your Caliph, here I am, if you have better man to be your Caliph, elect him and replace me". The people in one voice cried out— "O Umar Bin Abdul Aziz, we have full confidence in you and we elect you as our representative". Thus confirmed and elected as peoples representative, he went to mosque with three bags of title deeds and documents before the assembled persons and cut to pieces all title deeds and documents of his vast landed properties and estate.

Then he declared: "O people, documents represent usurped property illegally taken away from owners, I restore all these properties to their rightful owners.

9. He sent edicts to all governors to restore usurped properties. On his accession as Caliph he returned to the public treasury, all his personal properties, belongings, all parapharnalia of royalties, keeping only the royal shirt and also asked his wife to return similarly all jewellery and rich presents given by his father to the public treasury. He even dispensed with all servants and guards when he lay on his death bed, his woollen shirt was not washed for three days as it could not be changed for he had no other shirt. He ordered that the horses of the royal stable should be auctioned away and the sale proceeds should be deposited in the public treasury.

10. When one of his family members found him dejected and weeping, he enquired of him the cause of such weeping. He replied: "Do you not think, one who has been entrusted by Allah with the welfare of the vast concourse of people in the nook and corner of a vast empire and has been overcast with burden of great responsibility should not be sorrowful to think he would have to give relief, comfort, happiness, justice and security to every man of his vast relam."

11. Umar even returned the wedding ring to the public treasury. His favourite servant Mazhir once said to him: "What have you left for you?" Umar cried out: "Allah and his Prophet and nothing else." Such was the spirit and confidence of Umar in Allah and the teachings of the Prophet. He gave up the palatial building of former caliphs and lived in a tent so that all people may meet him easily. He never used Royal Building at Khorasan. He spent only two dinars a day. Before his election the income of his private property was fifty thousand dinars a year, but it was reduced to 200 dinars a year during his caliphate.

UMAR'S MANY SIDED REFORMS

12. He introduced many reforms—administrative, fiscal, educational, political—few of them were:

> (i) Under his order his Governor Assamah carried a census in Spain, not only of population, but also of the nature of soil, varieties of productions, of agricultural and mineral resources.

> (ii) The money of the Baitalmal which used to be used for the personal benefit of the caliphs ceased to be used so. He never drew a single pai from the Baitalmal for his personal use. He separated the accounts of Khiraj, Sadaqa and Fail.

13. His most important reform was in the field of taxation. He reformed land and taxation on a most just and equitable basis, and abolished all exactions and illegal levies. His fiscal reform proved so successful that revenue increased overnight, people became contented and happy, peace, order and prosperity ruled everywhere. There was no rebellion or disturbance and war during his caliphate. Even Kharijis were satisfied with his just rule. So also the Shiahs. Even oppressive Hajjaj could release 1½ crores as revenue from Iraq. But it increased to 11 crores during Umar's rule.

14. He reformed jail and ordered his Inspector General of Prison Ibn Hazur to visit jails weekly. Jailers and wardens were strictly ordered not to misbehave with prisoners. Every prisoner

was given monthly stipends and seasonal clothing. He arranged for the proper education of jail prisoners, so that they might come out of jail as useful citizens.

15. He built thousands of inns and sarais, public wells, charitable dispensaries throughout his empire. He adminstered justice tempered with mercy.

UMAR'S EXEMPLARY LIFE

16. Umar was an able administrator and followed the footsteps of the second Caliph Umar. He was a hard worker. According to Imam Sufian Suri Umar was one of the five pious Caliphs of Islam. He was very just and kind and tolerant to all non-Muslims. In Damascus the former Caliph broke down the baslica of the Church of John the Baptist and included the site in a mosque. Umar ordered the return of this site to the church, on complaint. Once a Muslim murdered a non-Muslim, he ordered the Muslim murderer to be executed.

17. Umar was a typical Muslim. He has shown by his life example that the principles of Islam, if applied correctly will solve many knotty problems of the modern world.

18. It is record that once he was deeply engaged in file work in his chamber, his wife Fatima wanted to consult him on an urgent matter. He asked her to bring his private lamp and to talk with him. Historian Ibn Saad says: "He never did his private work with the light of a lamp which was burnt by the state oil". This historian further records that once he used a small official paper for his private use but he soon returned similar paper.

19. He took ordinary coarse diet of common men. He never built a house of his own following the holy Prophet's example. He was a loving father, a patron and beneficent ruler of his people. He never accepted any presents or gifts. Once a person presented him a basket of apples but he returned it to him saying it would be bribery for him. He had profound faith in God and never cared for his life. Unguarded and without any protection he roamed about the streets hearing complaints from common men and helping them.

20. His instructions to his governor show his real character and his instructions were in these words: "Thou must know that the maintenance of religion is due to dispensation of justice and benevolence. Do not think lightly of any sin, do not try to depulate any place which is populated, do not try to exact thing from the people which is beyond their paying capacity and take from them what is just and equitable, do you utmost to ameliorate people's conditions and to increase their prosperity and happiness, govern justly, mildly and without oppression, do not accept any present even on festive occasions, impose no tax on travellers or on the marriages".

21. Umar Bin Abdual Aziz died in 719 A.C. having ruled 2 ½ years. He was really an ideal Caliph and a model ruler and a veritable beacon light among the rulers of the world. His words in his first address to the people are recorded in golden letters in histories. He said : "I am not better to any other among you. The only difference is that I carry greater burden of caliphate on my shoulder. Remember, no good comes out of disobedience of Allah's law. O people obey me so long I obey Allah, and if I disobey Allah, disobey me."

22. The exemplary life conduct of Umar Bin Abdul Aziz presents of picture of Islam in practical working. Umar's reforms in the fiscal field is worth imitation even in this twenty-century economic advancement. Umar reigned only 2 ½ years but during this short period he worked miracles in every field by his great zeal and indomitable faith in Islam and its principles.

◆◆◆◆◆

III

HARUN-AR-RASHID   (786-814)

1.   We are familiar with the name of the Caliph of Baghdad, Harun-ar-Rashid, "Hero of Arabian Nights". Most of us have most probably heard some romantic stories about Rashid. Arabian Nights contain one thousand and one stories and Harun is the hero of these stories.

2.   Upon the death of his brother Musa Al Hadi he was proclaimed Caliph in 786 A.C. According to the request of Caliph Mahdi, Rashid was very carefully trained by his father in the general learning, Military Arts, and State Craft. The stories of the Arabian Nights has cast a hallow of romance around his name. He has been represented as a romantic Caliph who used to go out by night to roam the streets of Baghdad to give relief to the oppressed and to remedy injustice. Rashid was decidedly one of the great monarchs of the world.

3.   Faithful and very particular in the observance and performance of his religious duties and obligations, austere and abstemious in his life, unostentatiously pious and highly charitable, yet fond of surrounding himself with the pomp and insignia of grandeur. Rashid exercised a great influence in society. He was a soldier by instinct and training. He participated in many battles personally. He travelled throughout his vast empire several times to personally learn the true conditions of his subjects and to redress their grievances. He personally inspected all frontiers and passes to ensure that frontiers and passes were well and effectively guarded against his enemies.

4.   He spared no labour and hard work for himself in the work of his administration. His most able and efficient administration

established peace and order throughout his wide empire. The merchants, traders, pilgrims, travellers, all enjoyed perfect immunity from danger throughout the length and breadth of his vast caliphate. He took keen care and interest in the welfare of his people and established schools, colleges, madrassahs, mosques, inns, caravan, sarais, hospitals, dispensaries, roads, bridges and canals in the whole of his empire.

5.   Rashid was a great patron of art and learning. He was always surrounded by a brilliant gallaxy of scholars, poets and scientists and men of great learning. His caliphate is characterised for the general prosperity of the people, for the unprecedented progress in art and science and for the brilliant culture and civilization of his reign. The glory and renown and fame of his reign were mostly due to the ability, wisdom and management of the officers to whom he entrusted the government of the empire. He and his ancestors Saffah and Munsur were fortunate in having Khaled Bin Barmek—a brilliant genius as their vazier and adviser. Khaled's son Yahya Burmakide was entrusted by Caliph Mahdi with the education of Rashid. Rashid made him his vazier and counseller when he became Caliph and was led by his advice.

6.   The Vazier Yahya's adminstration was wise, firm and benevolent; no detail, however minute was neglected and the well being and welfare of the people was made a prime duty of the administration. Yahya's sons namely Fazl, Jaafar, Musa and Mohammad were also men of great ability and administrative capacity of high order and they were governors of the provinces. For seventeen years his talented family governed the vast empire of Rashid with fidelity. But this gifted administrator fell from power due to palace intrigue.

7.   **Rashid's Empire**

During the caliphate of Rashid, the Muslim empire reached its zenith. Africa became an autonomous principality. The whole of Kabul and Sanhar was annexed to the empire, and the Frontior of the empire extended to Hindukush. Rashid repelled Khazars invasions of Armenia a barbarian horde—with iron hand.

8. Rashid's War with the Byzantine Empire

The Roman Empress Irene was succeeded by Nicephorus. He broke the peace established between the Muslims and Irene, and sent an insulting message to Rashid in these words: "Verily the Empress who preceded me gave thee the rank of a roak and put herself in that of pawn and conveyed to thee many loads of wealth and this through the weakness of women and their folly. Now when thou hast read this letter of mine, return what thou hast received of hit substance, otherwise the sword will decide between me and thee". Rashid was much enraged at this insult and simply replied on the back of the letter: "Verily I have read thy letter; the answer thou shalt behold not hear". Rashid was as good as his words. He started the same day with his army, and did not tarry on the way until he reached Heraclea, one of the Byzantine strongholds.

The boastful Nicephorus met the Caliph and his army was signally defeated and prayed peace agreeing to pay larger tributes to the Caliph. But the treacherous Greek again broke the treaty and invaded Muslims. Rashid, regardless of hazards of a winter expedition turned back and defeated Nicephorus to his great amazement who again made peace by agreeing to pay still heavier annual tributes and presents. But he again and again violated his treaty but each time he was defeated by Rashid and Rashid had to conquer more and more provinces of the Byzantine empire.

9. Rashid, while on an expedition to suppress a rebellion in Khurasan, fell ill seriously in a village named Sanabad near Tus. Feeling that his end was coming, Rashid sent for all members of his family who were in the army and addressed them thus: "All who are young will get old, all who have come into the world will die. I give you three direction: Observe faithfully your engagements : be faithful to your Imams (Caliphs) and unite among yourselves". He then gave a large largesses. Two days after Rashid died in the prime of his life on a Saturday the 4th of Jamadi II, after a glorious reign of twentythree years and six months.

10. An Estimate of His Character and Rule

Consider him in whatever way we like but Harun-Ar-Rashid

will rank with the greatest sovereigns and rulers of the world. Though in possession of despotic powers, he was self-restrained, devoted to the advancement of public prosperity and was very careful of the interests of his subjects. He never allowed himself the smallest respite in the discharge of his duties. His motto was vigilance and for this purpose he visited seventeen times all the places of his empire to see with his own eyes the conditions of the people, even in the remotest corners of his empire, to redress their grievances and to do justice. Nine times he himself led the caravan of pilgrims to the holy cities to show the value of Islamic solidarity.

11. Rashid's court was the most brilliant of the time; to it came the scholars, learned men, poets, philosophers, savants of great repute from all the parts of the world, and he always entertained and patronised them with large charity and stipends. He extended his unstinted patronage to all branches of art and science, and to all branches of mental study. He was the first to elevate the music into a noble profession establishing degrees and honours, as in science and art. In his reign the Hanafi School of Law began to take definite shape. Rashid extended the department founded by his grandfather Mansur for the translation of scientific work into Arabic. Rashid, says Ibn Khaldun, followed in the footstep of his grandfather, for no caliph exceeded him in liberality and munificence. Himself a poet, he was specially liberal to poets.

12. Communication were opened in his reign with West and the Far East. He was the first to receive at his court the embassies from the Emperor of China and Charlemagne and from other countries.

IV

CALIPH AL- MAMUN

1.   The Caliph Mamun-ar-Rashid was born in the year 170 of the Hijira, on the very day, his father ascended the throne. Mamun reigned twenty years and six months. While encamped in the vicinity of a place called Bedandur, not far from Tarsus he was attacked with violent fever and was brought to Tarsus where he died shortly after.

2.   In his last instruction to his brother and successor Mutasim: With his last breath Mamun enjoined his successor carefully to guard the interest of his subjects, to protect them from oppression, to do justice and never to transgress the law in the punishment of offence.

3.   Mamun's Character as Caliph

Mamun was the most distinguished of the house of Abbas for his prudence, his resolve, his kindness and judgement, his sagacity, and awe-inspiring aspect, his intrepidity, majesty, and liberality. He had many eminent virtues of head and heart.

4.   Mamun's caliphate was the golden epoch of Islamic history. His age has justly been called the "Augustan age of Islam". The twenty years of his reign have left the indelible monument of the intellectual developments of the Muslims in all directions of human thought and activities. These achievements were not confined to any particular branch of art and science, but ranged over the whole course of the dominion of intellect. Mamun's reign ushered in, as it did, the palmy days of literature, science and philosophy. He was himself a poet. At his court were munificiently entertained men of science, letters, poets, physicians and philosophers. Besides philologists and grammarians, it was also the age of the collectors

of traditions such as the great Bukhari and historians as Waqidi who wrote the most trustworthy life of the holy Prophet, and doctors of law as Shafi and Ibn Hanbal, speculative philosophy and belles letters were cultivated with as much care as exact sciences, mathematics, astronomy, the science of medicine and all made gigantic stride during this augustan age of Islam.

5.   Mamun's intellectual heritage flowed both into Muslim Spain and Christian Constanmtinople whence it descended to modern Europe. Mamun thought that the true happiness of his people lay in education and culture. He created permanent endowments for promotion and support of education and culture on a permanent basis. Oelsner very aptly remarks: "We see for the first time, perhaps in the history of the world, a religious and despotic government allied to philosophy, preparing and partaking in its triumph".

6.   In his broad tolerance Mamun recognised no distinction of creed or race; all his subjects were eligible for public offices and every religious distinctions was done with.

7.   Mamun established a regular Council of State, composed of the representatives from all communities, Muslims, Jews, Christians, Sabeans and Zaroastrians to adivse him in the administration.

8.   Liberty of conscience and freedom of worship have been always enjoyed by the non-Muslims under the Muslim rule under Mamun, the liberality towards other religion was large hearted. In his reign we hear of eleven thousand Christian churches besides hundreds of Synagogues and fire temples.

9.   In his knowledge of the traditions and jurisprudence Mamun excelled most of the doctors of law, his study of the Quran was profound and careful, he was a disciple of Imam Ar-Razi from whom he imbibed his love for philosophy and science.

10.   Mamun's reign was the most brilliant and glorious of all in the history of Islam. To him belongs the glory of completing the work of translating books of science, art and other rare books into Arabic from other languages, Greek, Latin, Persian, Sanskrit, Pali

etc. In his love for knwoledge he went so far as to exchange his rich territories conquered from the Byzantine for valuable books and manuscripts found in various libraries of the Roman empire. As soon as books were brought to Baghdad, they were translated by competent scholars and issued to the public.

11. The astronomical observations made in Mamun's reign in connection with the equinoxes, the eclipses, the apparitions of the comets and other celetial phenomena were most important. The size of the earth was calculated from the measurement of a degree on the shores of the Red Sea—this at a time when Christian Europe was declaring the flatness of earth. In his reign Abul Hassan discovered telescope.

12. Tuesday were set apart for literary, philosophical and scientific discussion in his palace and scholars and savants attended such discussion and were lavishly entertained. Mamun was extremely humane and he never imposed any punishment unless required by circumstances.

13. Mamun was extremely clever and tactful and had a unique genius of governing the people. Once a Kharijite Zealot came fearlessly near him and saluted him. Then he asked him— "O Caliph, tell me regarding this seat which thou occupying—doest thou sit at it with the unanimous consent of the people or by violence or force?"

Mamun at once replied: "Neither the one nor the other; but one who governed the affairs of the Muslims entrusted to me and to my brother. When authority came to me I felt I needed the unanimous consent of the people, but I saw that if I abandoned the government, the security of Islam would be disturbed. There would be anarchy and disorder, bloodshed, chaos in the empire of Islam therefore I arose in defence of the people until they should accord upon one man whom they should approve and then resign the government to him and I will abdicate in his favour."

The man replied: "Peace be to you and mercy of God and His blessing", and he departed. It was discovered that he was the leader of a band of Zealots who intended to rise against Mamun.

14. Mamun reigned twenty years. During his reign Mamun put down insurrections in Egypt, Asia Minor and other places. He defeated the Byzantines at battles. The Island of Crete was conquered in 825 A.C. and Sicili in 823 A.C.

15. Mamun married Busan, the most beautiful daughter of Hassan with great pomp and elclat. Mamun's reign still remains the Golden Age of Islam, not only in intellectual field but also in economic prosperity. The commercial life at centres of Mamun's empire was so developed and the state of trade was so flourishing that the entire capital of certain merchants consisted of valuable carpets alone which could be locked up in a small single room or it consisted of precious stones of rare value whose total cost of the whole stock exceeded several hundreds of thousand dinars. At Baghdad itself there were special markets reserved for one or other sort of commodity or goods and there were rows and rows of splendid arrays of gold and silver materails, jewels, china-wares, leather work etc. in that particular market where such articles were exclusively sold. So Mamun was the augustan kernel of cultural progress.

MAMUN'S ADVICE

6. "Be gentle and mild to others." Once Mamun-ar-Rashid the Caliph advised a person who used harsh and hard words. The Caliph said: "Please be mild in your speech". He further said: "Allah sent Moses and Harun, who are much better than you, to Pharoah and they were commanded by Allah. Speak to him mildly, perhaps he may accept your wisdom" (Quran 20-24). The Prophet said "If a Muslim does not help another Muslim whose honour is at stake Allah will never help the former when he will need his help."

V

ABDUR RAHMAN AN NASIR

1.   When Abd-ur Rahman III succeeded his grand father Abdullah in 912 A.C., he was barely twentythree years of age, but he proved himself the man of the hour. His were those qualities of resoluteness, daring and candour which characterise leaders of men in all ages. Abdur Rahman slowly and surely recovered the lost provinces, one after another with characteristic energy, which he displayed throughout his long reign of half a century (912-961), he extended his conquests on all sides.

2.   Eciza was the first to surrender and that on the last day of 912 A.C. Elvira followed suit. Jaen offered no resistance. Archidona agreed to pay tributes. Seville opened the gates towards the close of 913 A.C. Regio, whose mountain fastness had shielded the bold follower of Ibne Hafsun, was reduced step by step. Only Toledo remained unsubdued, but in 932 A.C. the former capital succumbed to famine and seige. Thus the whole Spain was pacified and the state consolidated under the sway of Abdur Rahman, most beneficent and benevolent ruler.

3.   In the mean time external foes were threatening him. Among them most dangerous were the Muslim Fatimids to the south and the Christian kings of Leon to the north. Realising that his position in Spain could not be safe when an enemy flourished in Africa, Abdur Rahman, whose suzerainty was recognised in Morocco early in 918 A.C. obtained possession of Centa in 931 A.C. and ultimately secured homage from a great part of the Barbary coast. His enlarged and renovated fleet, second to none in the world of that age, with Almeria as chief harbour, disputed with the Fatimid navy the supremacy of the Western mediterranean.

4.   While these operations against internal and external enemies were in progress, Abdur Rahman had to wage a holy war against the Christians of the north who had hitherto never been subdued. Here the land of the Basques occupied the centre bordering the Pyrenees. To east still lay the kingdoms of Navarre and Aragon. To west lay those territories which later on developed into the kingdom of Castile and Leon.

5.   These Christians from the north had been raiding the Muslim territories from 914 A.C. yearly. In 920 Abdur Rahman took the field in person, met the combined forces of Ordono (King of Leon), and Sancho the Great ruler of Navarre and inflicted on them a crushing defeat and overran parts of Navarre and near Christian lands and put an end to further Christian raids from the north.

6.   The remaining years of Abdur Rahman's long reign was marked by wise administration. In 929 he issued a firman assuming the title of al-Khalifah al-Nasir li-Din Allah (the Caliph, defender of the religion of God). He had still to fight against the Christians whoever had their covetous eyes on the rich land of the north. His campaigns against the Christians of the north continued upto 939 A.C. At the battle of Alkhandak the Caliph's army triumphed over the combined forces of Christians. At this battle the Muslims suffered great loss but Abdur Rahman's courage and energy did not damp in any way.

7.   Abdur Rahman continued his war against the Christians. In 955 Ordono III, son of Ramise had to sue for peace and a treaty of peace was concluded between Abdur Rahman and Ordono III. The brave Abdur Rahman had to wage war against the Christians till his death. But in every battle he was successful. As a result he crushed down Christian resistance. Navarre became a dependant state and Sancho invited his help and Sancho was helped by Abdur Rahman.

8.   The great Caliph enjoyed his success only for two years, for he died on October 16, 961 A.C. at the age of seventythree after a reign of a full fifty years.

9. The great secret of success of Abdur Rahman was in his frank, human, just and chivalrous behaviour with his troops. In April, 913 he appeared personally among his troops. The frank and chivalrous manners of the handsome Caliph and his desire to share with them not only their glory but also their fatigues and perils evoked extraordinary enthusiasm among his soldiers and exercised a wonderful influence on their morale. Another secret of his success was he was just to all.

10. Abdur Rahman's court, Al-Zahra at that time was one of the most brilliant in Europe. The Envoy from the Byzantine Empire and also from the monarchs of Germany, Italy and France were accredited to his court. Its seat, Cordova, with half a million population, seven hundred mosques, three hundred public baths, numerous schools and colleges was as grand as Baghdad and Constantinople.

11. Royal palace:

The royal palace (Al-Zahra), with four hundred rooms and apartments housing thousands of servants and guards stood northwest of the town on one of the spurs of the Sierra Morena overlooking the Guadal Guivir. Abdur Rahman began its construction in 936 and named it after his wife Al-Zahra (she with the bright face). It had columns and basis with golden statues 10,000 workmen with 1,500 beasts of burden laboured on it for a score of years.

12. Abdur Rahman's character and achievements:

Abdur Rahman an-Nasir was the ablest and most talented of all the Ommeyade kings of Spain. He had found his kingdom in a chaos, torn by factions and parcelled among a number of feudal chifetains belonging to different races, a prey to anarchy and civil war and exposed to continual raids from the virile Christian tribes of the north. In spite of great odds he had saved Andalusia and made it greater and stronger than it ever was before, Peace, order, prosperity reigned throughout his empire. The police arrangement was so perfect that any traveller, trader, even a woman could travel with perfect safety and immunity from danger throughout his empire including most inaccessible regions.

13. **Prosperity and happiness of the people and the country:**

  i   Agricultural development:

> The cheapness of all market goods, the excellence of the clothes worn by the peasantry, and the universal habit of riding even by the poorest testified to the general prosperity and happiness of the people. The smiling fields, the charming gardens, well stocked granaries, and a great wealth of fruits spoke of the wonderful impetus given to agriculture and horticulture by liberal aids by Abdur Rahman's Government.

  ii   Irrigational development:

> The splendid hydraulic work and the most unique scientific system of irrigation which made most sterile land fertile, evoked the admiration of the then world.

  iii. Development of Commerce, Industry, Arts and Science:

> It was not agriculture alone that was fostered by an-Nasir. Commerce, industry, the arts and sciences were patronised and developed. Cordova, Almeria, Sevelle and other cities had many special industries which enriched the population and added to the wealth of Spain. The extension of commerce was so extensive that custom dues alone supplied the major portion of the state income and it amounted to twelve million dinars.

14. **Abdur Rahman's Military Power**

The military resources of Abdur Rahman were formidable. He had a splendid navy and a numerous and well-disciplined army the best in the world according to historian Dozy.

15. The great rulers of Europe courted his alliance, and the Emperor of Constantinople and other kings of Europe established diplomatic relation with Abdur Rahman by sending their Ambassadors.

16. A Historian's Estimate

A well-known historian has made the following estimation of Abdur Rahman III:

"But what excites the admiration and wonderment of the student of this glorious reign is less the work than the workman. This sagacious man who centralised, who founded the unity of the nation and that of the monarchical power, who by his alliances established a kind of political equilibrium, who, in his large tolerance called to his councilmen of every religion, is especially a king of modern times rather than a ruler of the middle age".

17. Abdur Rahman was just and impartial. Abdur Rahman's one son attempted a resolt and was sentenced to death. His brother heir apparent threw himself with tears at the father's feet to cancel the sentence passed by the councel.

"As a father I shall shed tears of blood all my life", said the old Caliph, "but I am a king as well as a father; if I interfere in this case in the administration of justice, the empire will fall to pieces"— such stern and impartial was his justice in his time.

18. Never before was Cordova so prosperous, al-Audalus so rich and the state so triumphant as in the region of Abdur Rahman an-Nasir, and all this was achieved through the genius of one man. But this was the monarch who said in reviewing his long life that he could only remember fourteen days of unalloyed happiness in the whole of his life.

VI

AL RAZI (1149-1209) A.C.

1. The full name of Al Razi is Fakhar-al al Din Abu Abd Allah Muhammad bin Umar bin Al Husain. He was a famous theologian and philosopher of religion. He was born in Al Ray in 543 A. H. (1149 A.C.) and his father Deya-al-Din Umar was Khatib at Al Ray.

2. Razi's Early Life

After studying in his native town and in Maragha under the erudite teachers, he served a Shaf'ite and Asha'ite scholar. He then went to Khwarizm and then went to Bokhara and Samarkhand. In 1185 he worked in Ghazna and Hend, and finally settled in Herat under the protection of the Ghorid Sultans and the Khwarizm Shah Ala' al Din. In Herat a madrassah was founded for him where he as a famous scholar with the title Shaikh al-Islam attracted great masses of disciples. He died in Herat in 606 A.H. (1209 A.C.)

3. Al Razi was one of the most celebrated and notable theologian-philosophers. His life work is of important for his attempt at reconciliation of philosophy and religious traditions, in which he has shown a rationalism uncommon for his time.

4. To his first period of life belong his well-known treatise "Shah al-Isharat", a commentary and al Mabahith al Mashrikya.

VII

AL RAZI (RHAZES 865-925)

1.   Before Al Razi the theologian-philosopher, Abu Bakr Muhammad Ibn Zakaria Al Razi was born at the very place of Al Ray, called Al Razi after the name of the place of his birth. This Al Razi was most original of all the Muslim physicians and was one of the most prolific as an author. He selected a site for a hospital at Baghdad and he sought for a cooler site and determined it by putting fleshes in different sites.

2.   He was the inventor of the section in surgery. The Fihrist gives a list of one hundred and thirteen major and twentyeight minor works by Al Razi, of which twelve deal with alchemy. One of his principal works in alchemy, the Kitab-al-Asrar (the book of secrets), after having passed through many editorial hands was translated into Latin by Gerard Cremona in 1187 A.C. and became a chief source of chemical knowledge.

3.   While still in Persia he wrote a monumental work in ten volumes, named after his patron Kitab-al-Mansuri. It was published in Latin in fifteenth century. Parts of it have been recently translated in French and German languages.

4.   Among his monographs, one of the best known is a treatise on small-pox and Measles-al, Judari W-al Hasbah. It is rightly called an ornament to the medical literature of the Muslim. In it we find the first clinical account of small pox. Translated into Latin in 1565 and later in other modern languages this treatise served to establish Al Razi's reputation as one of the keenest original thinker and greatest clinicians, not of only Islam but of the world.

5.   His most important work was Al-Hawi (the comprehensive book). It is a veritable encyclopaedia, wide and rich in the range

of medical knowledge. It was translated into Latin under the
auspices of Charles I of Anyou in 1279 A.C. and under the title
"continens" it was repeatedly printed from 1486, a fifth edition
appearing in Venice in 1542.

6.   Printed when printing was still in its infancy, these medical
works of Al Razi exercised for centuries a remarkable influence
over the mind of the West. He was at first the State Doctor of Rayy
and later on he was appointed the chief physician of the Government
Hospital at Badad.

7.   He was an expert in surgery and cured many incurable
diseases. He made extensive researches in the diagnosis of various
diseases and his medical knowledge was acquired both theoretically
and experimentally.

VIII

SULTAN MAHMUD OF GHAZNA
(971-1000)

1.   Sultan Mahmud the Great was a great conqueror and a very learned Sultan of the 11th and 12th centuries. He played a most important role in the early Muslim history of Asia and India. Though his father Subaktagin laid the foundation of the Ghaznivide Empire, it was Sultan Mahmud who was the real founder of the vast Ghaznivide Empire. He also prepared the field for the establishment of the Muslim Empire in India.

HIS EARLY LIFE

2.   Mahmud was born in November 971 A.C. His mother was a daughter of the Amir of Zabulistan. He received education and training at the hand of a great scholar. He became well versed in various branches of litcrature. He was a Hafez-Quran and a profound scholar in the Sharia, Quran and traditions. His father himself taught him state craft, principles of good administration and these principles are embodied in the book "Pandenama."

3.   He was appointed governors of several provinces by his father Subaktagin during his life time, and thus received practical training in state craft and administration. So he was well equipped to play his role as a great hero of Islam. He was in some respect greater than Alexander or Nepolian.

4.   Sultan Mahmud's reign was one of the most brilliant in the history of Asia. He bcauitfied Ghazni. He was a patron of learning and arts, and his court was the resort of famous scholar and savants. Al Beruni, Ferdausi, Dakiki and many other philosophers and poets flourished in his reign.

5.   Sultan Mahmud's good name and brilliant life career has been much blackened, misrepresented and distored by some prejudiced historians, both Muslim and non-Muslim. He has been depicted as a great bigot, a zealot, a robber, a scourge of humanity, prototype of avarice, a breaker of Hindu temples and idols, a breaker of promise and even as a drunkard.

6.   Sultan Mahmud was a pious Muslim and his religious policy was based on Islamic teaching of toleration and Quranic injunction: "There is no compulsion in religion". He did not force any Hindu to adopt Islam and he never killed a person for the sake of his religion. The famous historian Elphinston writes—it is nowhere asserted that he ever put any Hindu to death except in battle or the storming of a fort." S.M. Haig in Cambridge History of India writes— "Though jealous of Islam, he maintained a large body of Hindu troops and there is no reason to believe that conversion was a condition of their service."

7.   Under Sultan Mahmud Hindus enjoyed perfect religious freedom and the Hindus were appointed in responsible posts. Tilak Rai, Soni were some of his Military officers. He did not make any distinction between Muslims and Hindus. Out of his seventeen invasions of India two were against the Muslim princes and others were against Hindu Rajas, and all his central Asian military operations were against the Muslim. If he invaded the Hindu Rajas he similarly invaded the Muslim Kings of Iran and Transaxiana.

8.   He was never led in his invasion of India by a desire to spread Islam in India or by a spirit of Jehad as some Muslim historians in their zeal to extol him have shown him to be. He was well versed in Quran and strictly followed Quran's injunctions.

9.   His policy in destroying some temples with idols was political, as these temples were used as forts and fortified places, and the Hindus resisted his onward march from these fortified temples. He never destroyed other temples. Dr. Ishwara Tope in his book "Politics in pre-Mughal Times" at pages 46-47 testifies to these facts in these words: "It may also be observed that the temples of India which Mahmud raided were store-houses of wealth and some of these were political centres. The temples were

in fact broken during the campaign for reasons other than religious, but in times of peace Sultan Mahmud never demolished a single temple". Even at his capital Ghazni Hindus enjoyed full toleration and Hindus were given separate quarters in Ghazni, and were allowed to observe their religious rites and ceremonies.

10. Sultan's life ambition was to establish a central Asian empire, but Jaipal, Raja of Waihaud, compelled him to attack him in India as Jaipal twice invaded Ghazni to conquer it. So his first invasion was due to Jaipal's action.

11. Sultan was equally eminent as a highly learned and cultured scholar and a great lover of learning and the learned. His achievments in the fields of peace, art, culture, science, and spread of knowledge was as great as that of Caesar, Augustus, Caliph Haroon-ar Rashid, Mamun-ar Rashid, Hakam. Sultan Mahmud was a fine poet and a great patron of letters. The literary renaissance of Iran was largely due to his munificence. His bounty and patronage attracted a large number of scholars, poets and philosophers from all parts of the world to his capital Ghazni which became a centre of light and learning. Whenever he conquered a place, he sent best book there—from his libraries in Ghazni. M.Elphinstone aptly remarks in history of India at page 290: "He showed so much munificence to individuals of eminence that his capital exhibited a greater assemblage of literary geniuses than any other monarch in Asia has ever been able to produce."

12. The names of some of the learned who gathered at Ghazni under Sultan Mahmud's patronage were—(1) Abu Nasr Muhammad, a famous historian; (2) Abu Rehan Muhammad bin Ahmad, a most eminent scholar, author of famous work Tahqiqi Milat Hind; (3) Al Farabi, the famous philosopher; (4) Abu Ali Sina (Avecenna), the greatest thinker and physician; (5) Abdul Malek bin Muhammad, the learned author of a metrical history of Iran; (6) Ferdausi, the famous poet; (7) Ansuri, the philosopher, linguist and the scientist; (8) the poets Dakiki, Asjudi, Marvi, Farukhi, Tirmizi and Menuchehar Balkhi.

13. Sultan Mahmud established many maktabs, madrassahs, colleges, mosques, museums and libraries. He constructed "celetial

bridge", a mosque of matchless beauty and grandeur, built of marble and granite at Ghazni, furnished it with golden and silver lamps and costly carpets. In the vicinity of this mosque Sultan established a big university and attached to it a huge library and a fine museum. Round the mosque there were three thousand quarters for the residences of teachers and students of the universities. The teachers were paid regular salraies and the students were given scholarships and stipends from the State fund.

14. We have read in most of history textbooks that Sultan Mahmud promised to Ferdausi to give a gold dinar for every verse of the Shahanama to be composed by him that when Ferdausi presented Shahanama to him be offered to pay silver coin for each verse in place of gold dinar that the poet was heart broken and wrote satyre calling Sultan a bastard and that Sultan sent the promised dinar to the poet while in death bed and his daughter received the same.

15. These are myths invented by figment of imagination by some of his enemies, many years after his death and have been so repeated that generally they are believed as true.

16. The whole story is concoctions, pure, simple and an after-thought invention firstly because there is no slightest reference whatsoever to this story in any of the histories and writings of the contemporary, Arab and Persian historians and by-writers who left detailed account of Sultan's reign. Secondly the Persian historian Aini, a contemporary of Sultan and his bitter critic does not mention this legend in his history— "Al Hind O Malahun Min Maqala Maqbul. Had these stories been true he would have surely mentioned them with glee. Thirdly there are many other histories of his time in which no mention of this story is made.

17. Then how this legend was invented ? One hundred fifty years after Sultan's death Nazami-al Aruzi in his book "Chahar Maqala" invents this story for the first time but he has not mentioned his source of authority or information. From him this malicious story has spread and found place in subsequent histories and books. Even the real author of Chahar Maqala is in doubt and various manuscripts found are full of contradictions. Fourthly all

the available source of this story are discrepient and contradictory on vital points. Even the name, nativity, parentage, dates of birth and death of Ferdausi, commencement and completion of the Shahanama, Ferdausi's age, education, life, even the number of verses of the Shahanama, the circumstances and events of Ferdausi's access to Sultan, Mahmud's order to compose Shahanama, the presentation of the Shahanama to Sultan, his perfidy, final repentance are differently given in different books and are also conflicting and self contradictory (vide literary "history of Persia" by Blowne vol II page 129). Fifthly Ferdausi himself wrote that Shahanama was completed in 400 A.H. = 1010 A.C. and that it took him 30 to 35 years to complete it. So it is evident from Ferdausi's own statement that he commenced Shahanama either in 365 or 370 A.H. that is two or three years before Sultan Mahmud asccended the throne. So the story of Sultan's order to compose and presentation to him fall to the ground.

18. So we see that the Shahanama was not composed according to Sultan's order and under his promise. Even Chahar Maqala does not say that it was composed by Sultan's order. So this legend about the breach of promise by Sultan Mahmud is not a fact, and the writing of a satyre by Ferdausi against the Sultan is not a fact. The satyre attributed to him is an after invention.

19. The story about Sultan Mahmud's breaking the idol Lingam in the Somnath Temple and the priests' offering to the Sultan gold and silver if he did not break the idol and the saying of the Sultan that he wanted to be known as an idol breaker than as an idol protector is not also a fact as it is not mentioned and recorded by the historians and writers who have recorded minutest details of the conquest of Somnath and it has been proved that this Lingam was made of solid and was not hollow, and could not be broken and no treasure could come out of it.

20. We now see how great and learned was Sultan Mahmud and how false legends have been created to *badnam* him, a most enlightened and true Muslim king of Asia.

His crying in the death-bed seeing his vast wealth and treasure out of feeling of avarice and love of worldly wealth is similarly malicious. The Sultan was a great learned savant and a most pious Muslim. He wept at the idea that all human greatness, power, wealth and life are transitory and fade away, but alas, men pride in them and forget Allah and disobey His injunctions.

21.   There are many stories about his sense of justice, human greatness.

Once a common man forced his way to Sultan Mahmud and said, "O Sultan, you are our ruler to protect us. One powerful soldier forcibly enters my house, spends his nights at my bed, he does not care for me". Sultan asked him to inform him when he came next in his house.

22.   One day this man again came to him and informed the Sultan that the soldier had come in his house. Sultan at once went with his sword in hand with the man to his house and asked him to put out light. He entered the house and killed the soldier found in his house with his sword. Then he asked the owner to light the lamp. He examined the man killed by him and raised his hands towards heaven and expressed his gratitude to Allah, and asked the owner to bring some food and drink. When the owner brought his coarse food and drink, the Sultan eagerly ate it and drank water.

23.   The owner of the house was simply amazed and enquired from the Sultan the cause of his strange conduct. The Sultan replied, "O my subject, I have been made your ruler by Allah to protect your life, honour, and property. When you complained to me three days ago, I felt great distress and since that day I did not take food and water till I do justice today. I was afraid that the culprit was my nephew, but I detected him not to be so. I conveyed my gratitude to Allah, and as I was hungry too much I asked you to bring food and drink, and I ate and drank so eagerly. You do not know how uneasy is the man who wears the crown."

Such strong was the sense of justice in the Sultan. We will find no such case in the modern days.

24.   Once Sultan Mahmud went to pay a visit to the great saint Shaikh Abul Hasan. He erected his tent in nearby village and sent

a message to the saint to meet him. The great saint refused to come out to see him and said, "I am a Muslim and I fear none except Allah. I do not fear his creatures however powerful. I have no time to obey the order of a king".

25.   The Sultan, though most powerful, was not enraged at the refusal of the saint and he himself went to pay his respect to the saint, and when he met he asked him to give him some admonition. The saint advised him— "Live a pure and honest life, fear Allah, pray in mosque, help the needy and love your subjects, do not wrong and injustice."

26.   The Sultan placed a large bag of money at the feet of the saint and requested him to accept it. The saint gave him a coarse dry bread. The Sultan tried to eat it, but he could not. The saint smilingly said "As you could not eat my dry bread, I can not accept your money. Take it, and spend it on your needy subjects."

Such was the Islamic spirit of humility in the Sultan, which is commendable.

27.   When the powerful Sultan Azdud Dowla died, his son was a minor and his mother ruled his kingdom Iraq as regent of her son. The Sultan made preparation to invade Iraq. The boy kings mother sent a message to Sultan in which she stated— "Had your message to surrender been received when my husband was alive, you would have received his brave response, but alas, my husband is dead now. My son is minor, and I am a helpless woman. I have heard that you are brave and chivalrious Sultan. It will be no honour, no chivarly and bravery if you attack a minor ruler and his helpless mother and conquer our country, but if you lose the battle, you will be humiliated at the hand of a woman."

28.   The Sultan received the message in brave spirit and his feeling of chivalry was uppermost and he did not attack the woman, and sent a message to her that so long her son was minor her country was safe from his attack.

Such chivalrious was the brave Sultan Mahmud.

29.   One day the Sultan looked at his face in the mirror and

found that his face was most ugly. He felt great shame. He said to his Vazir "O wise man of my realm, the people look upon the face of their Sultan for good fortune. I find that my appearance is most ugly and my people will not be happy at looking at my face."

The Vazir replied— "O Sultan and my master, it is not good look that counts but it is inner virtues which make a man, a ruler great and charming though his look is not so beautiful. But you possess in abundant degrees of those good qualities and virtue of head and heart. You are God-fearing, you are pious, you are just, you are learned, your inner heart is lighted with the light of learning, you are a Hafiz-e Quran, you are well well-versed in Quran and tradition, you are a man of character, you are just and impartial, you patronise learning and the learned men, you are tolerant and impartial to all. O master, be not grieved. Allah has endowed you with great gifts and talents."

IX

IBNE-SINA (980-1037 A.C.)

1.   Abu Ali Al Husain Ibn Abd-Allah called Ibn-e Sina was born in 370 (980 A.C.) at the little village of Afshana in the province of Bokhara. His father Abdullah, a native of Balkh was appointed governor of an outlying district of Bokhara by the Samanid ruler Nuh II Ibn Mansur. His grandfather's name was Hasan. Ibn-e Sina had a half share of Persian blood in him from his mother whose name was Sitara (Star).

2.   About early life of Sina, he says in his autobiography..... "I was born in Afshana and later we moved to Bokhara. By the time I was ten I had mastered the Quran and a great deal of literature, so that I was marvelled for my aptitude...... Then there came a man called Abu Abd-Allah al Natili who claimed to be a philospher. My father invited him to stay in our house hoping that I would learn from him also. Before his advent I had already occupied myself with Muslim jurisprudence, attending Ismail ascetic. He marvelled at me and asked my father to engage me in learning."

3.   Ibn-e Sina or Avecenna was one of the greatest and most original thinkers produced by Islam. He largely by virtue of his own exceptional genius and diligent self-instruction became a master alike of the ancient Greek learning and the Arab sciences and was author of large works in medicine and philosophy which translated into Latin continued to be studied in the Medieval universities of Europe.

4.   The most illustrious name in Arabic in medical annals after Al Razi is that of Ibn-e Sina (Latin-Avecenna, through Hebrew Aven Sin), called by the Arabs Al-Shaykh Al-Rais (shaikh and prince of the learned). He spent all his life in the

eastern part of the Muslim world, and was buried in Hamadan where his grave is still seen. In 1951 his millennary was celebrated throughout the Muslim world.

5.   As a youngman he had the good fortune to cure the Samanid Sultan of Bokhara Nuh Ibn Mansur and was given the use of the ruler's vast library. Endowed with uncommon powers of absorbing and retaining knowledge Sina devoured the content of royal library and at the age of 24 years he was in a position to write books. Alqifti lists only twentyone major and twentyfour minor works of Ibn-e Sina. Other titles increase the total to ninetynine, dealing with philosophy, medicine, geometry, astronomy, theology, philology and art.

6.   Of Ibn-Sina's works his best known poetical production is a lengthy ode describing the descending of the soul into body from the higher atmosphere and this book is still memorised by young students in the Arabic world. Among his scientific works the leading two are the Kitab-al Shefa' (book of healing), a philosophical encyclopaedia; and Al-Qanun Fi al-Taibb, comprehensive medical treatise. This Qanun or canon with its encyclopaedic contents became very famous in the medical literature and displaced the works of Galen, Al Razi and al Majusi and was a textbook for medical education in the schools of Europe. It materia medica contains seven hundred and sixty drugs. From 12th to 14th century Qanun served as chief guide to medical science in the West. It passed through many editions in many languages. In Al-Shefa Sina included a study of music.

Avecenna was undoubtedly one of the thinkers and physicians the world has produced. He is honoured both in the East and West.

7.   Ibn-e Sina practised as a physician and was known as a great physician. He cured many people from their sufferings and incurable diseases.

8.   While Ibn-e Sina was the Prime Minister of Shahenshah Ala-ud Dawla, a prince suffered from mental disease mania. He used to say he was cow and asked people to kill him and eat his

flesh. He refused to take food and medicine. Ibn-e Sina was engaged to treat this prince. He listened to the illusion of the prince that he was a cow. Sina asked a servant to go to his master and tell him that a butcher has come to kill the prince. The servant gave this news to the sick prince.

9.   After a little while Sina with a man entered the room and cried out— "I am the butcher, where is the prince to be killed". The prince cried out— "Here I am, kill me". Ibn-e Sina laid his hand on the body of the prince and cried out— "Oh, it is a thin cow. I can not kill such a thin and lean cow. It must be fed well to fatten then I will kill it."

10.   Since then the prince ate heartily food and medicine, thinking that he would be killed as soon as he became fat. He gradually improved in health and was cured of his mental disease. We find from the above case that how cleverly Ibn-e Sina treated his patients.

11.   Ibn-e Sina was appointed as Prime Minister in Hamdan but when the army revolted against the ruler, he had to flee for his life. But a few years after Hamdan was captured by the Sultan of Isphahan. He came back to Hamdan and was appointed the chief physician to the Sultan and he continued in this post till he died at the age of 58 in 1037 A.C.

12.   Ibn-e Sina has aquired so much undying fame as medical scholar and as an expert and brilliant physician, that he is still remembered in the world. The picture or portraits of Al Razi and Ibn-e Sina adorn the great hall of the school of medicine at the University of Paris. This shows how well known and reputed he still is in the medical world.

13.   Gifted with uncommon power of assimilation and a great thirst for learning, the boy Ibn-e Sina mastered the content of the vast library of Nuh Bin Mansur and in 21st year of age he began to systematise the accumulated knowledge of his predecessor and put it in writing in his masterly way.

14.   In his Qanun Ibn-e Sina draws attention to the contagious nature of pthisis, spreading of disease by water and by soil. Ibn-e Sina also took great interest in mathematics. He invented an instrument similar to the vernur. He also made researches in velocity of light and sound.

15.   While attached to the observatory of Ala ud Dowla Kake-wiyeh of Isphahan he made some important observations and these observations have helped the modern astronomers to make new discoveries of stars etc. His Arjuza Fial Tibb is an Arabic poem consisting of 1336 verse and is most widely read poem in the Arabic world.

X

HAZRAT DATA GANJ BAKHS ALI HUJWAIRI (981-1072 A.C.)

1.   Hazrat Data Ganj Bakhs was a great saint, philosopher and a learned professor. His most renowned book is Kashf-ul Muhjub—a unique book on theology and love of God. This book is very widely read in the Islamic world.

2.   Data Saheb was born in 400 A.H. in a village near Ghazani. He and his parents came from a respectable Syed family. His parents were very pious and God-fearing Muslims. Data Saheb was brought up in a religious and learned surroundings. He died as a great Muslim saint at the age of 65 and was buried in Lahore where his magnificent tomb still exists.

3.   In his boyhood he was educated in a neighbouring school. His teachers were impressed at his wonderful aptitude and genius for knowledge and, at his power to absorb the same. He was deeply devoted to his studies and did not waste his time in gossips and vain talks like other children.

4.   From his early life he was used to deep religious thinking and meditation. He often spend his leisure hours on deep meditation on Allah and His deep wonderful creations.

5.   When grown up he travelled widely in those hazardous days in search of knowledge and learning, and visited many countries braving all dangers of journey and he met many learned men of those countries and discussed religious matters with them to gain greater knowledge and learning. He became the disciple of a great saint from whom he learnt much and travelled with him.

6. The Data Saheb was much profited by the companion of his Pir, the great Shaikh. While travelling to Damascus, his Pir Shaikh Saheb became ill and died in his lap.

7. Before the Shaikh Saheb died he gave his disciple Data Saheb his last advice thus: "We are accountable to Allah for all our actions here. Allah has enjoined us to forget and forgive and to do good to others to meet evil with something better, and not to be revengeful and not to think evil of others, to be kind and courteous to all to shun pride and prejudice and to adopt the badge of humility in all our dealings, to win hearts and confidence by honest dealings, and so on. So forgive if any body has wronged you in any way. If you can rise above all passions you would be the happiest in the world."

8. Ali Hudjwiri gave up his travel after the death of his Pir and came to India and settled in Lahore. He founded a college at Lahore which acquired name and fame and became a centre of learning. Students and scholars came to this college for study and get knowledge and instructions from the Data Saheb.

9. Ali Hudjwiri was a great theologian and Sufi. He wrote many books on traditions and Islam. His most famous book is "Kashf-ul-Muhjub", in which he has explained the functions of Ruh or human soul. This book is widely read.

10. He died in Lahore. Every year many thousands visit his tomb at Lahore and recollect his pious life and deep devotion to Allah and Islam, and of his great service in the cause of learning and piety.

11. Hudjwiri's great service to Islam:

Hudjwiri in his book Kashf-ul-Mahjub and in his other books protested against the wrong interpretation of mystic thought by the writers of his time. His book Kashf-ul-Mahjub is a valuable master piece dealing with the pathological situation of the society and mystic thoughts of his time. He explained the mystic and religious dogma according to the basic concept of Islam. He has attempted to fight against the fast losing touch with the inward spirit and life which make religion reality. The problem of his time was to find out means to preserve the faith without rending community asunder and the answer to this question was provided by Hudjwiri. This was his great service to Islam. He instituted the concept of charity and human kindness with an emphasis that he knew no better way of attaining to God than by bringing joy to human hearts.

XI

NIZAM-UL-MULK   (1018-1042   A.C.)

1.   We have heard the name of Syasatnama which was written by Nizam-ul Mulk in Persian. It is a code of conduct for kings and princes. It is said that Machiavelli based his famous book prince on this book of Nizam-ul Mulk. This book was a text book in Persian for B.A. classes during the British regime in India.

2.   His full name is Khwaja Hassan Nizam-ul Mulk. He was born in 1018 in Rudk, a village near Tus. So he is called Tusi. His parents were of noble origin. They gave him sound education in many subjects of arts, science, and law. He grew up to be a very accomplished youth well-equipped to play a great role in life.

3.   At that time, the powerful Seljuk Sultan Alp Arsalan, who defeated the combined larger forces of the Crusaders at the historic battle of Manzekart with a smaller Muslim force, and saved Islam; was the ruler of the Sejukite empire. Hearing of his great intellectual attainments he offered Nizam-ul Mulk a minor post.

4.   Nizam-ul Mulk had an ideal for his life and worked hard to gain this ideal. After his heavy official duties, he studied upto 2 p.m. at night the methods of good government and other important subjects. His greatest ambition in life was to serve his country selflessly.

5.   Tusi was all devoted to his duties and did not depend on others and leave anything to his officers under him. He looked to every details of his administration personally.

6.   He was a keen lover of knowledge and persued knowledge ardently. He was sharp-witted and for his cogent argument people

felt preasure in debate with him. Sultan Alp Arsalan was so much pleased with his work. That he soon appointed him, though young, his prime minister.

7.   Nizam-ul Mulk accepted his Sultan's honour with all the humility and modesty, and without any ostentation. He was practically given great power by the Sultan. But Tusi was an honest and upright man. He never used or abused these vast powers for his personal gain and wielded them with justice and equity. He placed his country's interest above his personal interests, and always used for the benefit of his country.

8.   Sultan Alp Arsalan's son Malik Shah when succeeded his father retained Khwaja Hassan Nizam-ul Mulk in the office of the Vizirate and invested him with the absolute authority under the title of Atabek (Prince Governor). No doubt Nizam-ul Mulk was the ablest minister and administrator Asia has produced.

9.   His works on administration and government form an enduring monument of his genius and capacity. Peace reigned throughout the vast empire of Malik Shah extending from the borders of China to the Mediterranean in the west, and from Georgia to Yemen in the south, mainly due to Nizam-ul Mulk's able administration.

10.   Nizam-ul Mulk proved worthy of Sultan's trust. He was all attentive to improving the conditions of the people in his charge. He helped and encouraged commerce, trade and industry, and worked hard to remove poverty from the people.

11.   Tusi was a good organiser. He organised a police force to keep peace and order. As at that time journey to Mecca and Medina was not safe owing to presence of robbers, he introduced an armed guard system to protect the pilgrims in their journey to Mecca and Medina. At his suggestion the calendar was reformed by a committee of scientist under the chairmanship of the astronomer royal the famous poet Omar Khayyam. This assemblage of astronomers corrected all errors by a computation of time "Which" says historian Gibbon— "surpassed the Julian and approaches the

accuracy of the Gregorian". The reformed era was named 'Jalalian' after the name of Sultan Malik Shah Jalaluddin.

12.   Nizam-ul Mulk was a very cultured and learned man. He founded schools and colleges in cities and villages and established universities at Baghdad and Nishpur called the Nizamiya which became famous centres of learning. He spent largest sum, both from the government as well as from his personal fund for the spread of education among the people.

13.   From his pen we have one of the most remarkable Muslim treatise on the art of government, the Siyasatnama which he composed as a result of competition suggested by Malik Shah. The Sultan requested his statesmen to give him in written form the benefit of their opinions as to the nature of good government. Nizam-ul Mulk wrote this world known book as suggested by the Sultan.

14.   Nizam-ul Mulk was known for his charity and generosity. He never refused help to a poor or a needy person. He was assassinated in 1092 (according some in 1091) while travelling to Baghdad by a follower of Hassane Saffa who was his class friend and had grievance against him.

15.   The story goes that Khwaja Hassan, the celebrated poet Omar Khayyam and Hassane Saffa were class friends and playmates. Once they were playing, they together took decision that in future life, if any of them would hold any high position of power he would share such position with the others. When Nizam-ul Mulk became a prime minister, he kept this boyhood promise and offered power and position to Omar Khayyam and Hassane Saffa. Omar Khayyam accepted the offer, but Hassane Saffa refused to accept the offer. So when he founded the Ismailia sect and made Almut in Persia his headquarter, he prepared some blind followers who would act according to his wish, and one of those blind followers was sent by Hassane Saffa to kill Nizam-ul Mulk.

16.   Nizam-ul Mulk was universally loved by both the common people as well as the great for his noble qualities and spirit of

justice. The guiding hand throughout the administration of Alp Arsalan and Malik Shah was that of their famous Vazir Nizam-ul Mulk (the organiser of the kingdom), one of the ornaments of the political history of Islam. For the twenty years covering the reign of Malik Shah, Nizam-ul Mulk had all the power centred in his hand while the Sultan had nothing to do.

The basis of Nizam-ul Mulk's eternal glory is his establishment of the first well-organised academies for higher learning in Islam. Particularly famous was his Nizamiyah founded in 1065-67 at Baghdad. One of its chairs was adorned by Al-Ghazzali.

XII

IBN RUSHD

1. Muslim Spain has produced some of the brightest intellectual genius of the middle ages. One of them was Ibn Rushd, better known as Averrhoes in the west. He is universally accepted as the greatest philosopher of Islam and one of the greatest thinkers for all times. Being a versatile genius, he influenced the course of though both in the east and the west in more than one domain of knowledge.

2. His life

Abul Wahid Muhammad Ibn Ahmad Ibn Muhammad Ibn Rushd was born in Cordova, the capital of Muslim Spain in 1126, A.C. He came of a famous Muslim family of Cordova which held the high office of the Grand Gazi for the last two generations, Ibn Rushd holding the same position in the third generation. His grandfather was the Imam of the Grand Mosque of Cordova, and his father held the high office of Kazi.

3. Ibn Rushd received his education in his native city of Cordova which was the highest centre of learning in the west. He was taught tradition by Abul Qassim. He learnt Fiqh from Hafiz Abu Muhammad, a reputed scholar taught him medicine. Ibn Rushd soon acquired great scholarship in literature, law, philosophy and medicine.

4. He was a contemporary of some of the out-standing thinkers of Muslim Spain including Ibn Zuhr, Ibn Baja and Ibn Tufail.

5. He was appointed the Kazi of Seville in 1169. In 1182 he was invited by the Al Mohade Caliph Abu Yaqub Yousuf (1163-84) to Morocco and he was appointed as court physician. When

Berber fanaticism burst forth he was banished to Lucena near Cordova, and all his invaluable books except the scientific ones were reduced to ashes in 1194.

6. After fanaticism ceased, he was again called to Morocco by Al Mohede ruler Yaqub al Mansur, but the great Muslim thinker did not live long and died on December 10, 1198 A.C. His age at the time of his death was 75 years of age.

7. Character of Ibn Rushd:

Ibn Rushd was known for his humility and hospitality. Being pensive by nature, he hated position and wealth. As a judge he was very kind hearted and never awarded corporal punishment to anyone. He passed most of his time in study and it was said of him that during his long life there had been only two nights when he could not study-one the night of his marriage and the other the night of his death. He made no distinction between friends and foes. He was a great lover of his native land and has praised it in his works.

8. Ibn Rushd's works:

Ibn Rushd who is considered Avecenna of the west, applied himself to philosophy, mathematics, medicine, astronomy, logic and Islamic jurisprudence. His writings cover more than twenty thousand pages. His most important works are on philosophy, medicine and Fikh. He was an eminent logist of his time and acted as a Qadi for long time.

9. Renan in his book Averrhoes (pages 58-79) has given a list of Ibn Rushd's 67 works which include 28 on philosophy, 5 on theology, 8 on law, 4 on astronomy, 2 on grammer and 20 on medicine.

10. He was an astronomer of great repute. He wrote Kitab Fi Harkat Al Falak, a treatise dealing with the motion of the sphere. He is credited with the discovery of sun spots.

11. Muslim kings, rulers, princes and governors and wealthy persons were patrons of learning and liberally spent on knowledge and learning. The Ommayyed Caliph of Spain Al Hakam was a

great patron of learning. Himself a scholar he founded a big library of more than 5 lakh of books including rare manuscripts and read all these books and wrote marginal notes. Ibn Rushd was also patronised by the Spanish Muslim ruler.

12. Ibn Rushd's chief philosophical work is "Tahafut-al-Tahafut (the incoherence of the incoherence)". Ibn Rushd's writings on philosophy had a deep influence over the Christian Europe and he still continues to be the most popular philosopher in the west. Even some European writers think that Ibn Rushd belongs to Europe and European thought rather than to the east. Averrhoism continued to be a living factor until the birth of modern science.

13. Ibn Rushd's opinion:

Regarding taqdir Ibn Rushd was of opinion that man was neither the sole master of his destiny nor bound by unalterable degree, according to him the truth lies in the middle. Human actions depend partly on his free will and partly on outside causes. These causes spring from laws of nature and God alone knows their sequence.

14. Ibn Rushd is called a rationalist by most non-Muslim writers. He tried to establish harmony between religion and philosophy.

15. Ibn Rushd was a versatile genius. He wrote twenty books on medicine including Kitab-al Kulliyat fil Tibb (general rules of medicine) better known as colliget in Latin (this book written before 1162 A.C. comprises seven volumes dealing with anatomy, physiology, general pathology, diagnosis, materia medica, therapeutics). He fully understood the function of retina. This book was translated into many European languages.

16. Many biographies of Ibn Rushd have been written. Ibn Rushd has said. "The tyrant is he who governs for himself and not for his people". His works exercised considerable influence on the Christian and Jewish thought. An European writer remarks: "The philosophy of Cordova and its great teacher Ibn Rushd penetrated to the university of Paris".

◆ ◆ ◆ ◆ ◆

XIII

AL GHAZZALI (1058-1111 A.C.)

1.   Abu Hamid Muhammad Ghazzali was born in 1058 at Tus Khurasan where he died in 1111 A.C. He was one of the greatest theologians of Islam and one of its noblest and original thinkers. As a boy he attended the village school of his own village. He was a greatly intelligent boy and was studious and took keen interest in every subject. While still a young boy he went to the Nizamiyah Madrassah at Nishapur and studied under a great teacher Al-Jurwain.

2.   From Nishapur he went to the court of Nizam-ul-Mulk, the Seljuk Vazir and was at his court as canonist and theologian until 1091 when he was appointed to teach in the Nizamiyah University at Baghdad. He taught and wrote in canon law. He was a great success as a teacher and had innate power to teach his pupils well his name and fame as a professor attracted students and scholars from many countries.

3.   After teaching a few years in Nizamiyah University Al Ghazzali became tired of teaching. He had a deep religious tendency and a great thirst for knowledge. So he left the college in search of knowledge and studies.

4.   Al Ghazzali went to Mecca and Medina on pilgrimage. He spent much time in prayer and fasting. He travelled extensively and met many learned men and learnt from them. He went to Damascus and lived there for some time. He wrote some books on religion at Damascus.

5.   After 5 or 6 years travel of different countries, he again came back to Baghdad and taught again once more in the Nizamiyah University.

6. Al Ghazzali's religious desire was very strong. He again left the university and came to Tus, village of his birth. He established a religious school there and spent most of his time on writings on religion and many other learned subjects. He wrote many books and his books are widely read in the world.

7. Al Ghazzali was considered to be an authority on Islam and he was called Hujjatul-Islam. He was loved by all learned and not learned for his great learning, kindness and great intellect and power of understanding.

8. Al Ghazzali died in 1111 A.C. at rather in early age, leaving an example of studious life, of great scholarship, large humanship, and devotion to Islam, and service to Allah.

9. Ghazzali's thirst for knowledge:

Al Ghazzali reproduced in his religious experience all the spiritual phases developed by Islam. He says in his own words......
"Ever since I was under twenty (now I am fifty) I have not ceased to investigate every Dogma and belief such was the unguenchable thirst of my soul for investigation from the early days of my youth, and instinct gifted by God."

10. His works:

Among his works, Ihya Ulumal Din (the revivication of the sciences of religion) is his master piece. His other works are Fatehat Al Ulum, Tahafut Al-Falasifah, Al-Iqtishad Fi-al Itiqad are well known. Of Al Ghazzali's numerous books only four or five were written in Persian. Two most important books in Persian are-"Kimeyae S'aadat (the alchemy of happiness) and Nasihat-al Muluk (the advice to kings).

In the latter book works Ghazzali addresses the rulers of Islam and urges, them to justice and purity. The Kimeyae S'aadat is a book of human conduct. The whole book is divided into four parts and deals with worship (Ibadat), conduct (Mamulat), deadly vices, etc. Ghazzali gives intense importance to the daily prayer. To him prayer is the pillar of Islam, the foundation of religion.

11. In the chapter under head human conduct, he discusses trade, commerce, laws of marriage, almost all aspects of human conduct and social relations-right of neighbour, upbreeding of children etc. Ghazzali comments on music and song is worthy of consideration.

12. According to Ghazzali deadly vices consists of ill-temper, anger, lust, love of money, pride, hypocrisy etc.

13. Ghazzali's view of this world :

Ghazzali lays stress on shortness of this life but he insists that not a single moment of life should be wasted, and he says that there are noble objects in this life and it is only in this world. One can make preparation for the next life knowledge and practice which one should obtain in this world are the riches that would benefit in the world to come. The means of life such as food, clothing, dwelling and marriage, provided they are just to meet the needs are essential to keep one proceeding on the journey of life. "What is essentially needed is not considered as worldly interests" says he.

14. Ghazzali's greatest service to future men:

Al Ghazzali has left a vast volume of original works for a long chain of future men for which he is considered "A testimony and ornament for future Islam". During his 55 years' life he wrote one hundred master pieces and original works by dint of sheer labour and studiousness.

XIV

SULTAN SALAH-UD DIN AYYUBI

1. In the history of human race we come across many great men who appeared in their own times but have not disappeared like a water-buble and have left their marks on the history of the world and whose greatness still survive and inspire men to be great and noble. Sultan Salah-ud Din Ayyubi, hero of the Crusade war, is one of such great persons. He was great not in nobleness, chivalry, bravery, piety, generosity and in character, but he was great in every inch as an ideal man.

2. Short Life Sketch.

Al-Malik-al Nasir Al Sultan Salah-al Din Yusuf was born in Takrit on the Tigris in 1138 A.C. of Kurdish parentage at a critical time of Islam when the Muslim world was brokent into pieces, forming petty kingdoms and had fallen from its glory and power. Sultan comes of a race which was devout Muslim with strong tradition of honour and chivalry and hospitality.

Salah-al din had a physical features of Kurd, fair skinned, his eyes were kind and the charm and joyousness of his soul was attractive. He was like a true Muslim was of contented mind and was reposed. He was a man of simple and unostentations taste and habit and he hated pomp, grandeur and luxury.

3. His father Ayyub gave him sound education and good administrative training. Sultan Salah-al Din owed his public life to his father and uncle Shirkuh-who were the trusted generals of the Muslim King Sultan Zangi and his son Sultan Nurud Din Zangi. Shirkuh conquered Egypt for Nurud Din from the Fatamides. Salah-al Din went to Egypt with his uncle Shirkuh and succeeded him as Governor of Egypt.

4.   Salah-al din ultimately became the Sultan of the vast empire of Nurud Din. He sincerely thought his duty to try to unite all the free small Muslim states into a great empire. He believed that it was his noble mission to unite all Muslims and Allah has destined him to do so.

5.   As his powers grew, his finer qualities and innate virtues also grew. Sultan Salah-al Din was really great, whereever there was dispute with Nurud Din's son, he offered him in a respectful letter, to restore Hama, Emissa and Baalbek but his offer was rejected with haughtiness. In a battle with him, Malik Saleh's forces were defeated. Thereupon Malik Saleh sought for peace and a young daughter of Nurud Din, a mere child was sent to the camp of Salah-al Din to incite his pity and to obtain favourable peace terms. Salah-al Din received this child with the greatest kindness, covered her with presents and at her request gave all the cities taken by him in the state of Allepo. This shows how great and noble was Salah-al Din.

6.   Salah-al Din's firm and grim resolve power of endurance and patience, his chivalry in victory and above all his character and honesty made him a true leader of the Muslims, and he fought and beat back the Crusaders who came to efface Islam and reconquered Jerusalem, Acre and other cities from the Christians. As a Muslim hero and an eminent general Salah-al Din was a most brilliant military leader in history. His victories against Christian Crusaders were won through his military genius, wisdom and personal examples.

7.   Sultan Salah-al Din was inspired by the life example of Nurud Din Zangi who in his life and government revived the zeal and simplicity of the first caliph. Even the Christians had to admire the wisdom, courage, the justice and of piety of Nurud Din, their bitter foe. Gold and silver was banished from his palace and wine from his kingdom. His dear wife once sighed for some female object of expense-"Alas", replied Nurud Din, "I fear Allah and I am no more than the treasurer of the Muslims. Their property I can not spend for you, dear wife."

His chamber of justice was terror for the great and the refuge for the poor. A few years after his death an oppressed man called out-"O Nurud Din, where art thou now. Arise, arise to pity and protect us". A tuemult was apprehended and a living tyrant blushed and trembled at the name of Sultan.

8.   Such inspiring example of his master inspired the every step of Sultan Salah-al Din, and moulded his character. Historian Gibbon writes about Salah-al Din in these words-"The garment of Sultan Salah-al Din was of coarse woollen cloth and water was his only drink. Both in faith and practice he was a true Muslim. At stated hours, five times a day the Sultan fervently prayed with his brothers. His reading of the Quran on horse back between the approaching armies may be quoted as a proof of his piety and courage. The justice of his divan was accessible to the meanest of applicant against himself and his ministers. He was affable and patient with the meanest of his servants. So boundless was his liberality, that he distributed twelve thousand horses at the seize of Acre and at the time of his death no more than twenty drahm of silver and one piece of gold was found in his treasury, yet in a martial reign the tributes were diminished and the wealthy citizens enjoyed the fruits of their industries. Egypt, Syria and Arabia were adorned with by the royal foundations of hospitals, colleges and mosques. All his works were consecrated to the public use. The Sultan did not indulge in a garden or palace. The genuine virtues of Sultan Salah-al Din commanded the esteem of the Christians. The emperor of Germany gloried in his friendship and the Greek emperor solicited his alliance."

9.   Non-Muslim writers and historians have called the Sultan Salah-al Din as great leader of Islam. In that dark age of enmity, barbarity, depravity, oppression and suppression Sultan Salah-al Din stood out alone refulgent and shining as a great leader and guide to the humanity.

10.   Sultan's great shining example:

(i)   When Renand, the Christian Lord of Sidon came to Sultan and pretended to become a Muslim to save his castle from his attack, Salah-al Din saw through the trick but he nobly pardoned Renand.

(ii) Sultan admired honours in others. He released the young
lord of Oultre Jourdain on the promise of boy's mother to
surrender the castle of the province. The garrison refused
to obey her order, so she sent her son back to Salah-al
Din but he released her son at once as a tribute to her.

(iii) Salah-al Din's still greater qualities were the mercy,
charity and chivalry he showed to his defeated enemies.

While Richard, the Crusading king of England had no hesitation
in butchering some 3,000 Muslim prisoners whose lives he had
sworn to protect; but the only Christian prisoner Salah-al Din slew
were French Renand and Knights of the temple, two in number.

When the Crusaders captured Jerusalem in 1099 A.C. they put
all the Muslim citizens including women and children numbering
more than seventy thousand to death and fire. But when Sultan
Salah-al Din recaptured Jerusalem in 1187 A.C. not a single civil
life was lost and not a house or a church pillaged. The Christians
were rounded up and held for ransom and he and his brother gave
help toward the ransom out of their own pockets and compensated
out of their own purse, Christian widows and children whose
husband died in the fighting.

11.   The story runs that a young Christian mother came weeping
to him in his camp before Acre and complained that the Muslims
had stolen her little daughter. Sultan himself searched the camps
and restored the daughter to her. A terrified Christian prisoner
afterwards said— "As soon I saw his face, I was comforted for I
knew that he could do no evil".

Sultan's Chivalry:

At the heat of the battle of Jaffa when King Richard's horse was
killed under him, Sultan Salah-al Din at once sent to him two swift
horses of his own and when Richard lay sick in his tent he sent him
fruits and snow.

The Sultan besieged the castle of Kerak and was bombarding
the castle, but when he learnt that the young Chatelain was

celebrating his marriage, he at once asked his forces not to bombard the tower in which the royal couple dwelt.

12.   When the Sultan lay dying, he had his standard bearer to go through the streets of Damascus carrying rags from shroud proclaiming this was the all that the great Sultan, Sultan Salah-al Din could take to his grave.

In February 1193 Sultan Sahah-al Din fell ill and died twelve days after at the age of fifty-five.

Thus died a great and noble Sultan. The measure of his greatness is that Christians and the Muslims then and now recognise his essential nobility. Salah-al Din's greatness deserve to be remembered. He fought with such compassion and such honour. He was more than a mere warrior and champion of Islam. He patronised scholars, encourged studies, built dykes, dug canals and founded schools and mosques.

We all should follow his example.

X V

MUIN AL DIN CHISTI (1142-1236)

1.   Muin al Din Chisti, founder of a Sufi brotherhood called Chishtiya is widely known in India and Pakistan and is one of the greatest saints of the world. He is called "Aftabi Mulk Hind (sun of the kingdom of Hind). His death anniversary or urs is celebrated every-year at Ajmir and Muslims and non-Muslims in great number gather annually at Ajmir on the occasion of his urs to show their respect to the memory of this great saint.

2.   Muin al Din Chisti belonged to Sistan. He was born in 537 A.H. (1142 A.C.). When he was fifteen years of age, his father Ghyath al Din died and some days after his mother also died. His father had a small garden by which he earned his livelihood. He had other brothers and this garden land was partitioned among all brothers. Chisti got a small share of the garden, the earning from which was inadequate to meet the cost of his living. So he sold away his share and gave the price to the poor.

3.   He left his birth place and lived in various towns of Khorasan. He came to Bukhara which was then a centre of learning and culture and while at Bukhara he studied deeply and greatly and became well versed in Quran and Hadis. Then he went to Nishapur which was another seat of Muslim culture and learning and acquired further knowledge in Sufism and Muslim theology. He finally came to Bagdad.

4.   During this period he came in contact of most famous Sufis of his time including Nadjim al Din Kubra, Shihab al Din al Suhrawardi and Awhad al Din Kirmani. At Nishapur he became a disciple of the famous Saint Othman Haruni and he lived in his society for twenty years and went with his Pir to Mecca and Medina.

5.   In 589 A.H. or 1193 he came to Delhi and from Delhi he went to Ajmir, and near a lake near Hindu temple he made his Astana. At that time Prithiraja was the Hindu King of Ajmir. His pious life and saintly character attracted to him many Hindus many of whom embraced Islam at his hands. There was a Hindu agitation against him but his great faith in Allah, firm determination to overcome all obstacles in the way of Allah ultimately won the day and he was allowed to stay in Ajmir.

6.   Muin al Din Chisti spread Islam in India against many odds by his life example. He died at Ajmir in 1236 A.C. and was buried there. A grand mausoleum was erected over his tomb by Sultan Muhammad Khilji of Malwa. His tomb at Ajmir became a popular place of pilgrimage. Emperor Akbar made a pilgrimage to his tomb on foot. A splendid mausoleum or dargah was erected which is much visited to this day.

7.   Muin Al Din Chisti brought the Chistiya order in India. His khalifa was Khwaja Kutbal Din Kaki buried near the Kutb Minar in Delhi and his khalifa Baba Farid Shakarganj (D 1268 A.C.) whose shrine is at Pak Pattan in Montgomery (Punjab).

8.   Practice of Chistia Brotherhood :

They lay special stress on word-Illa, lllah; use vocal music in their religious service and wear coloured clothes dyed.

9.   We know the famous tradition of the holy Prophet. He did not like pure and simple asceticism and prayed to Allah not to make his tomb a place of worship as the followers of other religions have made their Prophet's tombs a place of worship.

10.   Muin al Din Chisti was a great saint and pious soul. He taught many thousand Muslim and non-Muslim by his life conduct the true religion of God. He was a great learned scholar deeply versed in Quran and Hadis. Even his daughter was a great literary genius.

◆◆◆◆◆

XVI

ABDUL KADIR GILANI (1078-1166 A.C.)

1.   Abd-al Kadir al-Djili (Gilani) Muhyil Din and Sufi, after whom Kadiria order is named was born in 470 A.H.-1077-8 A.C. and died in 561 A.H.-1166 A.C. He was born in the village of Nif or Naif in the district of Gilan, south of the Caspian. He was sent to Bagdad at the age of 14 years. He was born at a critical period when there was depression and spiritual decline and the political Islam was tottering.

2.   According.to some writers he was a descendant of Hazart Ali,-ten generation from Imam Hasan and fourteen generation from Imam Hussain, but according to others he was not Quraish but an Azmi. His father was Abu Swaleh (father of virtue) a very pious man and his mother was Fatima, daughter of Saiyyid Abdullah Saumai, a well known saint of his time. She was a very pious lady and accomplished woman of her time.

3.   At the age of 17, when he acquired all the knowledge available in Gilan, he made up his mind to go to Bagdad then a famous centre of learning for the whole world in those days. After obtaining his mother's permission who was his only guardian then, he proceeded from Gilan to Bagdad with a merchant's caravan.

4.   His mother taught him to speak the truth always and to be upright and honest in all his dealings. The healthy influence of his pious and wise mother played a great role in his after life.

5.   While he was about to start for Bagdad his mother sewed in his under garments thirty gold dinars for his expenses at Bagdad and advised him to speak the truth and never lie.

6.   While the merchants' caravan with which Abd al Kadir travelled was in their journey, a gang of robbers attacked the merchants in the way and ordered the merchants to handover all their valuables. Some of the merchants tried to hide their valuables. The boy Abd-al Kadir standing alone. Some of the robbers went to him if he had any valuable thing with him he replied that he had thirty gold coins given by his mother. The robbers did not believe him and took him to their sirdar or chief. Sirdar asked him whether he had any thing with him. He again replied— "I have thirty gold coins with me". Then he asked-"Where they are". He said "Here sewed up in my inner garments" and pointed out the same. The robber was simply amazed and asked him— "O boy, while all are hiding their valuables, why you alone pointed out your valuable coins?" The boy Kadir replied -"O Sirdar, my dear mother ordered me to speak truth, nothing but the truth and never lie as Allah says in the Quran to speak truth against himself, even against father, mother and relations". So I have obeyed my mother's order.

The robbers were moved so much by the words of Kadir that they repented for disobeying Allah's command and gave up their profession of robbery.

We thus find that speaking truth how bears fruit and reforms human lives. The robbers restored to merchants all their properties and henceforth became God-fearing Muslim.

7.   At Bagdad Abd-al Kadir became a favourite pupil of Allama Tabrezi, the principal of Jamiah Nizamiah and studied there six or seven years and became accomplished in all branches of learning. His chief attainment was his mastery over Arabic language. He soon became a very famous orator. For his great learning Allama Saiyyid Ahmad of Bagdad entrusted him with the charge of his college where he taught innumerable students in fourteen branches of learning.

8.   The fame of his lectures spread over the whole Muslim world and his audience numbered 70 to 80 thousand listeners usually. Four hundred persons were to take down his lectures at the same time. His teaching and lecturing began in 521 A.H. and continued upto 561 A.H.

9.   His lectures and speeches were so effective that a large number of Christians, Jews and other non-Muslims embraced Islam and thousands of thieves, robbers and other criminals were reformed and turned into good persons. He did away with all undesirable innovations and irreligious practices in Islam. His services as a religious reformer was so great that he was given the title Yuhiyyuddin (the renovator of faith). He is also known as "Gousul Azam".

10.   By his ideal life example Abd-al kadir taught people to live better lives and think of others first and themselves last.

In 1134 he was appointed as the head of the school of Mubarak-al-Mukharrim. No better person could have been chosen for this high task. He was a great scholar and orator with vast knowledge in religious matters. He was kind and just. He never injured any body. His saintly character and noble nature and his teaching to help each other endeared him to all. Kings and leaders of all countries sought his advice on questions of religion and of law.

11.   He founded the Kadiria order. The saint died on Monday the eleventh Rabi-us Sani in the year 561 A.H. at the ripe age of 91 years.

12.   Abd-al Kadir's works:

Abd-al kadir's works are all religious in character and largely consists of reports of his lectures, sermons or addresses. The following are among his knwon works:

(i) Al Ghunya li Talibi Tarik al Hakk- A ritual and ethical treatise. (ii) Al Fath al Rabbani, 62 sermons preached. (iii) Futal Ghaib, 78 sermons on various subjects. It is a remarkable book in Sufism. In his works Abd-al Kadir figure as a capable theologian and an earnest sincere, and eloquent preacher. His doctrine is strictly orthodox and the tone uniformly sober and breathes a spirit of charity and philanthrophy.

13.   All over the world the Muslims who try to follow his noble

example by leading God-fearing lives and his missionary zeal are honoured throughout the world. By his selfless service and spotless ideal character and inspiring life example he has rendered great service to Islam and to the world.

14.   The Kadiria order has now been branched off into several sub orders in different parts of Asia and Africa. This order is most tolerant.

XVII

SULTANA RAZIA (1236-39)

1. Razia, daughter of Sultan of Delhi Altamsh Shamsuddin, who ruled Hindustan for twentyfive years, was the celebrated Queen of Muslim India. As the sons of the Sultan Altamsh were all dull and unfit to rule, Altmash trained up his daughter with special care in all branches of learning and state craft, horsemanship and art of warfare, and she grew up to be very accomplished lady well-qualified to rule over an empire after her father. She was most beautiful, charming and often dressed as male and rode on horse back.

2. Altamsh while alive declared her as his successor; but his father's nobles after the Sultan's death, raised his worthless son Rukúnuddin to the throne in 1234, but when he proved a failure as a ruler, the very nobles made him abdicate.

3. Razia ascended the throne of her father in 1236 in accordance with her father's wishes and eastern eyes saw for the first time the spectacle of an unveiled and crowned empress.

4. The beginning of Razia's reign was attended with much dangers and difficulties, caused chiefly by the refractory governors who hesitated to concede allegiance to a queen but however quiet was established throughout the empire and Razia's rule was acknowledged from Sind to Bangal, Daibal to Lakhnauti.

5. She was a very enlightened queen and felt for the people and took keen interests for the welfare of the people. She often appeared in male dress to perform office duties. She took keen interest in sports.

6. She was brave and courageous and expert in horsemanship.

She herself led the armies on horse back. At her accession when the governors rebelled she suppressed the rebellion with supreme courage and tact.

7.   She reigned only 3-1/2 years and would have ruled the vast empire with ability and success, had she been allowed to rule peacefully; but the jealous nobles and governors did not allow her to show her merit as a ruler.

8.   The nobles of her court, and governors here and there rebelled against her rule. Altunia, Governor of Sirhind rebelled against her. Razia marched out with her army to suppress his rebellion. The Afghan Turkhi nobles obstructed her way and made her prisoner. But she cleverly managed to escape and marched against Altunia.

9.   In the battle with Altunia's forces she had no success, and to obtain peace and order she married Altunia thinking that now she would be allowed to rule peacefully with her husband, but the courtiers and nobles set her brother Bahram against her and declared him the Emperor of Delhi.

10.   Razia and Altunia's forces were defeated by Bahram in a battle and both escaped for life but they were detected by the Hindu band and were mercilessly killed in 1240. Thus ended the life of a most enlightened and accomplished princess who ruled India.

XVIII

FARID-UD-DIN   SHAKARGANJ

1. Baba Farid-ud-Din Shakarganj who died in 1268-69 and whose shrine exists at Pak Pattan in Montgomery in the Punjab was a Khalifa of the Chistia brotherhood. The descendants of his relations and children have formed into a class which is found in the lower Satlej and chiefly in the district of Montgomery.

2. Baba Farid had two disciples, Ali Ahmad Sabir, whose shrine is at Piran Kaliar at Rurki and whose followers are known as Sabir Chisti: the other Nizamuddin Aulia (1238 to 1324) whose followers are called Nizami.

3. Baba Farid came from Kabul to Lahore and then shifted to Montgomery. Hazrat Khwaja Farid-ud-Din surnamed Ganje Shakar was the greatest mystic and spiritual preceptor of his age. He spent all his life in the service of Islam and to propagate Islam in India. His name and fame as a great sufi spread all over India.

4. A very interesting event took place. The great saint Nizamuddin Aulia was directed by Shaikh Najib-ud-Din Al-Mutawakkir to go to Ajhodhan (Pak Pattan) and sit at the feet of Hazrat Khwaja Farid-ud-Din.

Acting upon his direction Mullah Nizam-ud-Din at once started for Ajhodhan and when the great saint Baba Farid saw the Nizam-ud-Din he uttered this memorable verse: "Welcome art thou, the fire of whose separation has roasted the hearts of lovers, and the flood of whose love has totally devastated their souls".

5. Before Nizam-ud-Din could touch the feet of Baba Farid he embraced him warmly and forthwith placed his own cap on his head as an indication of his formal initiation in the holy Chistia order. Baba Farid gave him intense training and after the end of the training period he sent him to Delhi to found a khanqah to train preachers for preaching Islam.

6. Baba Farid's service to spread Islam is great and immense. He had a magnetic personality. People from all parts of India used to throng his abode at Pak Pattan. Princes, nobles, theologians and common people all listened to his spiritual speeches every morning and evening.

7. His bounty and munificence knew no bounds. Whatever he received in cash or kind he gave it away then and there, keeping nothing for himself. Many dervishes and mendicants ate at his table every day.

8. Baba Farid died in 668 A.H. (1268) and was buried at Pak Pattan in the district of Montgomery where his shrine still exists and is yearly visited by many thousands.

9. His important sayings:

  (i) Faith is Muslim's primary need.

  (ii) Faith is a ladder to the gate of reality and reality is nearness to Allah.

  (iii) Hold fast to the rope of faith and seek firmness at every stage.

  (iv) Verily faith without deed is a mere skeleton and deed without faith is chaos and confusion.

  (v) Welfare of Muslims should be considered in terms of faith.

  (vi) Muslims should have full faith in the Creator. They must not run after what is unreal and void.

  (vii) Be not disheartened for want of worldly requisites. If you are steadfast in the cause of Creator alone, He would provide all that you need. But if you pursue merely material requisites it would mean that you believe much in matter than in Allah's promise and powers.

  (viii) Sincerity of a Muslim drenched in the faith is essential while conducting assemblies for purposes of consultation.

  (ix) Remember, that pure faith of a person affects the minds of other people. Faith is strengthened by virtuous deed.

XIX

NIZAM-UD-DIN AULIA (1234-1325)

1.   The real name of Nizam-ud-Din Aulia was syed Muhammad. He was the son of Syed Ahmad. His ancestor emigrated from Bukhara to Lahore and finally settled in Badaun in the United Province of India. Nizam-ud-Din Aulia was born in Badaun in 634 A.H.

2.   His father died when he was five years' old. He was brought up under the fostering care of his mother. His mother was a very pious lady. She gave her son the best education available. After learning the holy Quran by heart, he began his studies in Arabic and Persian languages and fikh with great diligence and lobour. In his student life he exhibited his great devotion to studies and learning.

3.   He was intelligent and hard working and he had a great aptitude for knowledge. When he finished the study of "Quduri", the famous text book on Muslim Sharia or jurisprudence, it is said, his God-fearing mother invited all the leading ullemas to her house and requested them to wrap the academic turban round her son's head according to them custom.

4.   His mother took him to Delhi then capital of the Indian Muslim empire for higher studies in theology. He was taught theology by Maulana Shamsuddin and Maulana Kamal-ud-Din, who were the most celebrated ullemas of their time, and he acquired vast knowledge in theology. He mastered logic wonderfully and acquired the most uncommon ability for debate and discussion. For his vast erudition and great learning he was called Mulla Nizam-ud-Din Bahhas (the great debater).

5.   From this time he spent most of his time in service of Islam, propagating Islam in India. He went to Pak Pattan to meet Khwaja Farid-ud-Din Ganje Shakar, the greatest saint and preacher of Islam of his time. Ganje Shakar Saheb warmly received him and embraced him and placed his own cap (Kulahichahar) on his head as a token of formal initiation in Chistia order.

6.   When Nizam-ud-Din Aulia Chistia completed the period of his training with the Ganje Shakar Saheb, he directed his beloved disciple Aulia Saheb to go to Delhi to set up a khanqah to train preachers to preach Islam.

7.   His name and fame as a great saint spread far and wide, and he was given the title of "Sultanul Mushaikh" by his followers. He carried the order of his great pir and established a khanqah at Delhi. In time his khanqah became a centre of Muslim Missionary activities throughout Hindustan.

8.   He had a charming and captivating personality. The people from all parts of India, Muslims and non-Muslims, began to come to his khanqah in Ghayaspur-a suburb of Delhi. All classes of people, nobles, princes, learned ullemas, common people heard his speeches and sermons with great attention every morning and evening.

9.   His bounty and hospitality knew no bounds. Whatever he received by way of present or gifts in cash and kind, he forthwith gave the same to the poor and needy keeping nothing for himself. Many dervishes and mendicants were fed by him daily. He was a true Muslim Sufi and fully devoted to Islam and wholly relied on Allah.

10.   He never cared for wealth, power, position, and never feared any one except Allah. He was fearless and intrepid. Even he had no hankering to attend on kings and emperors of his time. The poet Amir Khusrau was his favourite disciple.

11.   Once Sultan Jalal-ud Din Khilji, emperor of Delhi asked Amir Khusrau to take him to Nizam-ud Din Aulia. Amir Khusrau promised to do so. He informed his master of the coming visit of

the Sultan to him. The great Aulia Saheb at once left for Pak Pattan to pay a visit to his Pir Ganje Shakar. The following day the emperor came to know about the sudden departure of the Nizam-ud Din Aulia and took Amir Khusrau to task. Such was the spirit of this great saint. He even did not care to meet the great Sultan, symbol of great power.

12.   Sultan Ala-ud Din Khilja, who was one of the mightiest emperors, who sat on the throne of Delhi tried to meet the Aulia but he could not succeed.

13.   The great saint died on Wednesday, the 18th Rabiul Awwal 725 A.H. (1325 A.C.) at the ripe old age of 91. Seven kings sat on the throne of Delhi during his life time but he never gave audience to any one of them, though all eagerly desired to meet him.

14.   A few hours before his death he appointed Nasir-ud Din surnamed Cherage Delhi (the light of the city) his khalifa or successor, and exhorted him to keep aloft the torch of divine faith, Islam, and to continue the noble mission of preaching of Islam in India. Then he commanded Khwaja Muhammad Iqbal, one of his companions to distribute away all the stocks of grains, cloth and other goods, necessaries of life among the needy and the poor. When this was done, he ordered him to sweep all the cells of langarkhana (general kitchen), and the khanqah (monastery) clean.

Then he said-"I do not want to go to my master and Creator Allah in the capacity of a man who owns earthly possessions." So I have given away all which Allah bestowed on me in His infinite mercy; as Allah commands in the Quran-"Give in charity out of what He has granted upon men. Do not be niggardly. Who is among you to give beautiful loan to Allah, Allah will doubly reward such loan".

15.   He has departed from this life no doubt, but his name is still alive and today every year thousands of Muslims and non-Muslims visit his shrine to show respect to the memory of this great man who lived and died for service to Islam and to hummanity at large.

XX

AMIR KHUSROO

1.   Amir Khusroo was not only a poet but also a first class musician. For many hundred years he has been a prominent figure for the common men and has been admired by them.

2.   He was an erudite scholar, a great poet, a shrewd statesman, a famous linguist, a humorous philosopher, a popular courtier, a charming debater and talker, and aboves all a great musician. He occupies for his many virtues a high place in the circle of the learned. His poetical genius has charmed all the lovers of poetry.

3.   Amir Khusroo was the third son of Amir Sherifuddin Mahmud who was a famous soldier and a courtier of the Delhi emperor Sultan Altamsh. His ancestors came to Afghanistan with the armies of Chengis Khan and from there migrated to India. Amir Khusroo was born in Patiah of Turbesh parents in 1255 A.C. His father wanted his son to follow his profession of a soldier. He was born in a very chaotic period of the history when petty princes were fighting and disappearing. He himself served several Sultans of Delhi.

4.   He followed in his early life the profession of a solider as desired by his father and fought many battles and by dint of merit he was promoted to the rank of an Amir or commander.

5.   The signs of his future greatness was visible during the reign of Ghyasuddin Bulban. His virtues and qualities made him an attractive figure at the court of Delhi Sultan. Sultan Kaikobad admired him most and he acted as adviser to him. During Sultan Alla-ud Din Khilji's reign he was at his full glory as a great literary genius and at that time he became a devout disciple of the great saint Nizam-ud-Din Aulia who moved from Ajodhan to Delhi

and settled in a suburb. The saint Nizam-ud Din liked Khusroo who could recite verses in Turkish, Arabic, Persian and Hindi.

6.   Khusroo in his book "Afzali Faward" has mentioned the incident of his meeting with the Aulia and in 671 A.H. became his disciple, Nizam-ud Din gave him the title of "Turki Elahi" or the sword of Allah. Nizam-ud Din loved Khusroo very much. When he became ill Khusroo was in Bengal. Hearing of the illness of his Pir, he hurried to Delhi but the Aulia died before his arrival. Khusroo was much shocked and mortified at his Pir's death and he himself died five months after in 725 A.H. or 1327 A.C. or according to Elliot in 1325 A.C.

Thus ended the life of a great man devoted to art and culture.

7.   Amir Khusroo was a brilliant scholar and a literary genius. He wrote volumes and was prolific in productions. Besides four diwans in Persian he wrote over ninety books as mentioned by historian Ziaud-Din Barni in his Tarikhi Feroz-Shahi. Some of his famous works or historical poems are: (1) Mutlai Anwar, (2) Eijazi Karulni in three volumes-Khalik Dari, Anasir Khusroo which contains seven thousand couplets. He also wrote a short history of 21 years' reign of Alla-ud din Khilji. His last production was the famous Masnavi Tughlagnama on Sultan Gyasuddin Tughlag. Besides these he composed many hundred couplets in Hindi, Turkish and Arabic languages.

8.   Khusroo as a Lyrical Poet:

As a lyrical poet he may be compared with Sa'di and Keats. His ghazals are extremely charming and popular. Shaikh Sa'di, master of lyrics gave him the title of "Tutiya Hind" nightingale of Hind.

9.   Khusroo as a musician:

As a musician Khusroo was not only a lyrical poet but he was also a successful composer of many other forms of poetry. His masnavies are great master-pieces. As a musician Khusroo excelled. The old form of Hindu music was mostly religious recitations. He made a revolution in Indian music and developed it into an excellent art. He introduced 'Khyal' type of singing. He gave new shapes to 'ragas'. Some of his well-known 'ragas' are Eaman, Sazgiri, Zeelaf, Gharia and Forghana. He introduced a new form of singing 'Tarana'. 'Goul' and 'Gabana'. He made great contribution to musical instruments. He introduced Sitar and a Tabala and Banya.

10. The full name of Amir Khusroo was Yamin-ud Din Muhammad Hassan. According to Cowell, he was born in 651 A.H. (1253 A.C.) and died in 725 A.H. (1325 A.C.). He lived in stirring times and was taken a prisoner by the Mughuls in 1285 A.C. and Khusroo secured his release with difficulties.

11. Khusroo's poems and other works:

His prose work Tarikhi Alai or Khazanul Futuh contains an account of Alla-ud Din Khilji's reign. His poem Keranus Godain (conjunction of two auspicious planetes) was composed to celebrate the meeting of Sultan Kaikobad with his father Nasiruddin Sultan of Bengal. His poem Ghurutul Kamal Miftahul Futub is a masnavi and his other poems are Nu Siphar (nine heavens), Ashika are historical poems.

12. Amir Khusroo left indelible marks on Indian music. He expressed in his works the consciousness of his age. For ages to come he will remain as one of the greatest creator of Indian art and culture, loved, admired and respected by millions.

Background of Khusroo's poetry is typically eastern and the frame work include the Muslim spirit. It contains aestheticism of Persia and the refined sensibility of Arab poetry.

So some of his ghazals still retain their freshness charm and appeal.

◆◆◆◆◆

XXI

SHAH JALAL TABREZI

1. Shah Jalal originally belonged to Tabrez, of which city he was also a governor. He was a disciple of Abu Sa'eed Tabrezi, the great savant and saint.

After the death of his great teacher and spiritual mentor, Shah Jalal installed his son in his own seat as governor and himself went to Bagdad, where he placed himself under the guidance of the famous Sufi Khwaja Shahabuddin Suhrawardy.

2. Shah Jalal's devotion to his teacher was deep and intense. Khwaja Shahabuddin was a very old man at this time and had to take food that was hot and soft. Therefore whenever he travelled Shah Jalal would remain attendance with him with a stove to serve a hot meal.

3. While Shah Jalal was studying with Khwaja Shahabuddin, a scholar from India also came for study and religious training with the same teacher. His name was Shaikh Bahauddin Zakaria Multani. Both became close friends, and a strong bond of friendship sprang up between the two. While Shaikh Bahauddin Multani was returning to India he requested Jalal to accompany him to India. At this time Shah Jalal came in contact with Shaikh Farid-ud din Attar, whose saintly character and life example left a deep impression in Shah Jalal.

4. Shah Jalal lived with Zakaria Multani for long, and they separated. After leisured travelling Shah Jalal came to Delhi. Sultan Altamsh then reigning Sultan came out to receive him. From Delhi he went to Badayun. In the vicinity of Badayun there were strongholds of a number of marauding robbers. These robbers were so impressed by the saintly life example and piety of Shah Jalal,

that they embraced Islam and gave up robbery and became good Muslims.

5.   From Badayun Shah Jalal travelled to Bengal for some time at a place called Dewa Mahal. Shah Jalal was burning with a desire to keep the torch of Islam burning in India.

6.   While in Bengal, he was astonished to see one day that his host got his son to have a careful bath and dress in his best, but he was puzzled to see that both mother and father were bitterly crying while dressing their son in best dress. He enquired of them the cause of their crying, and was told that under the order of the local Raja their son had to be sacrificed to a god who would come tomorrow.

7.   Shah Jalal pursuaded his hosts to allow their son to go with him to the jungle where the god-giant would come to take their son's sacrifice. At first they hesitated but ultimately agreed and allowed their son to go with him. To their surprise they found Shah Jalal and their son coming out of the jungle all hale and living.

8.   The story of this remarkable event spread far and wide. Many thousand Hindus came to him and embraced Islam. He visited Mando also where a number of people embraced Islam.

9.   Later Shah Jalal travelled to Mando (Central India) and he got a tank built and a number of gardens planted and attached a khanqah to these gardens.

10.   Shah Jalal passed away from this world in 642 A.H. or 1244 A.C. near Gohati in Sylhet and was buried. A magnificent shrine has been built over his tombs. Every year thousands of people visit his shrine at Sylhet.

11.   In Mando he has left a mosque and chillahkhana where his urs (anniversary) is held every year on 21 or 22 Rajab.

12.   He was the first Muslim missionary to enter Bengal to preach Islam. His preaching, his saintly character, his pious and examplary life, his selfless service to humanity, his charming personality, his humanity, his devotior to Allah, and his learning

and scholarship, and his zeal to spread Islam won the day, and Bengal, especially. East Bengal became prominently Muslims in population.

He has proved that the myth of spreading Islam by force is a cobweb of falsehood, and it is such saints and traders who have spread Islam by their own efforts in face of all odds.

13. Shah Jalal belonged to that band of the faithful who in the language of the Quran will ask the people to do good and righteous deeds, and to abstain from evil deeds.

XXII

IBNE BATUTA (1304-78 A.C.)

1.   From the earliest times Muslims have had yearning for travel and adventure. Islam has infused this spirit of travel by enjoining upon every Muslim to go to Mecca for pilgrimage at least once in his life. The Muslims braved all dangers and hardships of a travel. The modern world owe a great debts to Muslim travellers for much of knowledge about different countries during the past centuries. These adventurous brave Muslim travellers risked their lives and faced hardships to see for themselves what lay beyond their own countries.

2.   Abu Abdullah Muhammad surnamed Ibne Batuta is the greatest traveller in history. Ibne Batuta was born in Tangier in 1304 and died in 1378 at the ripe age of 73. His father Abdullah Muhammad was a poor man. Ibne Batuta's early boyhood was not easy one and he had to work hard for his daily bread. But he had intense thirst for knowledge even in his early life.

3.   He attended a village school and paid deep attention to his studies, while other boys spent their times in playing and looking at sights. He took keen interest in all subjects and particularly in customs and habits of other countries. His strong desire was to learn as much as he could about the way in which different people lived in other countries.

4.   The lust for wandering came to him when he was 21 years of age and for the next thirty years he was almost constantly on the move. In June 1325, Ibne Batuta set out for Cairo, then one of the greatest cities of the world. The journey was long and tiresome, and he felt very lonely and homesick.

5.   At Tunis, he says in his travel book: "There was no

salutation for me. I knew no soul there. I burst into a flood of tears. A pilgrim saw this. He came forward and did me courtesy, and he consoled me till I was housed in the city". Little human touches like this makes Ibne Batuta's travel record one of the most appealing books in the world. At Tunis he joined a caravan going to Alexandria where he reached in April. He saw the forests of masts in the docks of Alexandria, the great mosque of Cairo, the procession of the holy carpet going to Mecca, and many shrines of Muslim saints. He decided to go overland to Mecca after exploring Palestine and Syria.

6.   At Jerusalem he saw the great temple of Soleman the holy house which covers the rock whence the holy Prophet ascended the heaven on the occasion of Mehraj celetial journey. He describes Lebanon as: "The most fertile mountain on the earth, copious water springs and shady groves laden with fruits of all kinds." Here he met the sect of the assassins. Ibne Batuta now reached Damascus. He speaks of Damascus thus: The chief mosque was a most graceful building; he had ever seen and he visited the cave where Abraham was born and the Grotto in which Adam's son Cain betowed the body of his brother Abel.

7.   Ibne Batuta's travel is full of little humorous anecdotes. Here is one: At Damascus he attended a sermon by a popular preacher. The Imam was dramatic rather than orthodox in his methods. "God came down to the earthly paradise just exactly as I am descending these pulpit steps", he exclaimed suiting his action to his words. "It is a lie" shrieked a rival ullema and the excited congregation fell upon the preacher and beat him soundly.

8.   He joined a caravan going to Mecca from Damascus. The journey was an arduous and tiresome. The pilgrims saw on the roadside the bones of men and animals who had died of thirst and they heard the sound of ghostly drumming in the sandy wastes. Ibne Batuta reached Mecca and performed his first Hajj.

9.   From Arabia he travelled with the caravan to Iraq and Iran where he visited many interesting sights and places. In his journey to Iran he had to travel over six hundred miles of Central Arabian deserts. He reached the city of Meshed Ali not far from the site of

the battle of Karbala in the lower Mesopotamia. He says-"Here takes every year the famous night of revival. Invalids from all over the world are laid on the tomb of Ali. People then some praying and others reciting the Holy Quran. They all spring up cured".

10.   Ibne Batuta then travelled to Ispahan and Shiraj. His notes on then Iran is interesting. He found the Persians honest, virtuous, God-fearing folk. At Al-Hillah on the Euphrates he records a curious ceremony, the invocation of the unrevealed Imam. "Every day a hundred armed men came to the door of the mosque leading a horse saddled and bridled. They beat on drums and say aloud— "Come forth O lord of the times, for the whole earth is filled with evil doings and deeds of shame. Now hath the hour come for thee to reveal thyself so that through thee Allah may divide the truth from the false. In this way they wait until darkness drives them home."

11.   Ibne Batuta again performed the second Hajj and spent two years at Mecca studying theology.

In 1330 he set out once more on travel. He visited sea coasts and famous tanks. Everywhere he was welcomed. His notes are interesting. He writes— "Here the people are too fat. A single man eats as much as congregation". In 1333 he performed his third Hajj.

12.   Then he sailed down to the Nile to Cairo. He then travelled to explore Asia Minor and Southern Russia. He saw several petty states in Asia Minor. His account of these states has much of interest— "In each town was one or more clubs or guilds the members of which made it a point of honour to feed stranger feast them, even provide them with horse for journey".

13.   From Asia Minor Ibne Batuta crossed to Cuffa (Frodosia) in the Cumea. Cuffa was in the hands of Genoese merchants and Ibne Batuta who had never been in Christian town before, was sorely tried by continuous ringing of the bells in the church, a strange discordant sound to him.

14.   He now decided to pay a visit to the court of the mighty

Muhammad Uzbeg, the descendant of Chengis Khan and overlord of the Khans of Volga. He describes the great Khan's camp thus: "A city on wheels, complete with streets, mosques and cook houses. The Khan gives audience on Fridays. His four wives unveiled are seated on thrones on either sides with his two sons at his right and left hand and his daughter on front. Around stand princes, Amirs and other people in order of rank. When one of his wives enters, he rises and leads her to her seat".

15. Ibne Batuta was amazed at the shortness of northern nights. At one place which hevisited, during Ramadan, he had scarcely time of finish the unset prayer before midnight, while hurry as he might, he was overtaken by the dawn halfway through his midnight devotions. Silent barter trade was practised in Russia.

16. Ibne Batuta now resolved to cross Central Asia and visit India, touching on the way at Bokhara, Samarkhand and Balkh. His travel record of the little Khanate at which he stayed is full of interest. Their simple, old world piety greatly attracted him. At one place the Imam had a whip hanging at the door of the mosque. Those who failed to attend prayer were publicly whipped and fined. The money going to the upkeep of the building. At another place, the Khan sent word to the Imam that he would be late for service and desired that the prayer may be delayed. The Imam asked the Khan whether he or Allah had ordained prayers and bade the Muezzin to carry on. At the second prostration the Khan appeared and humbly joined in the prayer. Afterwards he shook hands with the Imam.

17. Ibne Batuta arrived through Turkistan in India in 1333 A.C. having crossed the mountains to which he is the first to give the name of Hindukush or Hindu slayer because of the vast number of captives who perish while crossing them. Ibne Batuta reached Delhi and entered the service of Sultan Muhammad Tughlag as a Kadi on a monthly salary of one thousand rupees.

18. In 1342 Ibne Batuta again became restless to travel. An embassy from the emperor of China visited Delhi and Ibne Batuta obtained permission to travel with the embassy to China. He travelled from Delhi to Cambay, then to Calicut to catch a Chinese

junk. However a disaster overtook him. The junk was wrecked and he was left stranded on the shore.

19.   Then he visited Maldive Island. About Maldive he writes— "Here is a land where it was always afternoon". He stayed here for a year. His account of Maldive Island has never been surpassed by any writer, old and modern.

20.   Ibne Batuta then visited Ceylon and made arduous climb up the great peak upon whose summit is "The foot mark of our father Adam." He then took ship to Bengal and landed at Chittagong. He then embarked on a vessel bound for Sumatra, a voyage of 40 days. At Sumatra he embarked on a Chinese ship and landed in a Chinese port. He writes that - "Though he was disgusted with the pork eating habit of the Chinese, China is the safest and pleasantest country in the world. Although it is a nine months journey from one end of the kingdom to the other, the traveller even he has no money, need he be anxious, there are officials with armed gaurds at each halting place."

21.   In 1346 Ibne Batuta set off home on his return journey. He once saw the mighty bird "The Rukh", flying with an island in his talons. He stayed at Cairo and made his fourth Hajj. He reached Fez in November 1349 and stayed there. But in 1352 he visited the capital, Cordova of the Moorish Muslim kings, and saw Gibralter. Then crossing channel he plunged into the worlds of Central Africa and saw houses built of rock salt and penetrated to Timbuctoo. In 1354 he returned and by royal roder he dictated his travel description to Muhammad Abu Tujai, the Sultan's Secretary. He died in his bed at the ripe old age of 73 in 1378 A.C.

22.   Ibne Batuta was a wonderful traveller, explorer and writter in Islam. He was equally at home at the courts of Uzbeg Khan in Russia, in Delhi or Peking, in Sumatra and Central Asia. He was a careful observer. He had a keen sense of humour and never failed to note down the whims and caprices of the people. He will never exceed the truth.

◆ ◆ ◆ ◆ ◆

XXIII

EMPEROR SHAH JEHAN (1628-57)

1.   Jehangir was succeeded by his son Shah Jehan in 1627. Shah Jehan ruled the empire upto 1657 and died in 1666, i.e. after about 30 years of his rule.

2.   Shah Jehan is best known in history for his architectural monuments and legacies. The intellect of Shah Jehan, the artist lover was claimed off by the art of architecture. In taste and talent, he was more akin to his grandfather than his own father. During the period of his education, his grandfather's tender care shaped his mind. Both grandfather and grandson fondly desired the continuance of Mughul rule in India, but Akbar wanted to perpetuate his name by founding his politicomystic faith "Din-E Illahi" and his grandson Shah Jehan wanted to commemorate his name through architecture. The builder of Fatehpur Sikri could be easily distinguished from the builder of Taj Mahal and Peacock Throne. The one was urged by his ambition to be great, the other, by his zeal to perpetuate that greatness. Ambition is the key note of the character of both. The one concealed his ambition in his practical politics and the other, in his love for art. So we find that, although Shah Jehan never grudged his patronage to other arts and learning, his love for perpetuation voted him off for the most lasting of these architecture.

3.   Shah Jehan left us nothing in the form of written work, like his father's autobiography. But we can base our judgement of his capacity and ability to write books from some of his stray writings. The first letter he wrote to Yameen-ud Daula Asaf Khan, after his accession to the throne is an ample testimony to his learning and power of expression. Beside this there are his discussions and his talks recorded in the book-"Amale Saleh" (Good deeds) which go to prove that Shah Jehan's learning was quite deep and his information and studies were vast and profound.

4.   Shah Jehan's pratical talents found another field of expression as well. It was history, a record of men and ages, and to his credit we read that he was dissatisfied with the standard of his court historian and he discovered the talents of Qazvini and entrusted to him the task of writing Badshanama. Badshanama written by Abdul Hamid Lahori is a detailed history of the first twenty years of Shah Jehan's reign. This history also embodies an account of the Princes of royal blood, of the nobles of Jehangir's court according to their rank and it also contains an account of the Shaikhs, learned men, poets, physicians etc. who flourished during Shah Jehan's reign. He also respected learned men and his great regard for Wazir Saadullah and Mullah Abdul Hakim reflects creditably on his intellectual standards.

5.   Shah Jehan was a great and powerful ruler. He suppressed with iron hand two rebellions of Janjur Singh Sarder of Bundela and of Khan Jahan Ludi. At that time the Portuguese traders were fortifying their trade-stations at Hughli in violation of terms of the treaty and were collecting illegal tolls from Indian traders. Shah Jehan checked all these Portuguese excess and violation with great strength. By suppression of all rebellions, disturbances, lawlessness, disorder he established peace, order and prosperity throughout his vast empire. Shah Jehan extended his empire upto the Southern India. According to the author of Shah Jehannama during Shah Jehan's reign. Tibet was conquered by Adam Khan and formed a part of the Mughul Empire.

6.   Shah Jehan personally checked the works of his officers and was a paragon of justice. He helped the poor orphans, and widows from his public treasury. He always redressed the injustice done to any one of his subjects.

7.   Shah Jehan was also devoted to education and founded a grand college near the Jama Masjid of Delhi and maintained it with liberal grants. An European traveller who visited Delhi during Shah Jehan's time found 24,000 books in the Imperial Library of Shah Jehan in 1642 A.C.

8.   Amal-e Saleh written by Mir Muhammad Saleh Kambu is an anthetic history of the reign of Shah Jehan from his birth to his

death in 1665 A.C. Shah jahannama by Muhammad Sadek Khan is another history book which records the history of the reign of Shah Jehan from the time of his accession to the throne to the time of his dethronement.

9.   Jehangir died in 1627 A.C. after reigning over twenty years. He was succeeded by his son Khurram who took the title of Shah Jehan (King of the World) as emperor. Shah Jehan was the most brilliant and the most magnificient of all of the Mughul emperors in India. He won many battles by showing superb military strategy and force of arm. He brooked no interference with his royal degrees.

10.   Bengal was occupied by Portuguese traders who oppressed the Bengal peasants. Shah Jehan sent an expeditionary force to Bengal and the Portuguese were turned out of Bengal.

11.   Shah Jehan's court was one of the unprecedented splendour and grandeur. Shah Jehan took his seat on the decorated and jewelled Peacock Throne, which was shaped and designed on the model of famous bird peacock. Not only was his court a brilliant spectacle of pomp and grandeur, it was also illuminated by the intellectual luminaries of that ages such learned scholars, poets, writers, musicians, scientists etc. who were the masters of that time.

12.   All the Mughul emperors were famous for laying out exquisite garden and superb buildings but Shah Jehan excelled and surpassed all the Mughul rulers in this respect. The Jama Masjid in Delhi, the Tomb of Jehangir at Shahdara and the Salimar Bagh in Lahore built during his reign are monumental works of architecture. The famous Taj Mahal at Agra built by Shah Jehan as a memorial to his beloved Queen Mumtaj Mahal is one of the wonders of the world.

13.   The beautiful Salimar Gardens which are situated five miles east of Lahore and by the side of the Grand Trunk Road was designed by Shah Jehan. It is the rare example of an unique park with terraces, tanks, canal designed and constructed on the model style of architecture. The garden is 1,500 feet in length and 690

feet in width and covers an area of 44 acres of land. The garden is surrounded by a high wall of fine brick work. The garden has two separate parts with three successive terraces. The first part with the first terrace is called Farah Buksh and the second part with the middle and the third terrace is named Faiz Buksh.

14. The gates of entrance to the garden which were used during the time of Shah Jehan lie in the western and eastern walls of the garden of the third terrace. The gates of entries which are used in present day lie by the side of the Grand Trunk Road and leads into the royal apartments.

The top terrace which leads into the main garden has a exquisite screen of marble work. On the top terrace lies the Baradari, a beautiful mansion with numerous open doors through which the cool breezes flows in and out. Two beautiful canals flow across the terrace and form a small lake in the centre.

15. Charming sandstone step at both end of the first terrace lead down to the middle terrace of the garden. This portion of the garden is most exquisitely and beautifully drawn up and present at artistic panorama to all visitors. Square water-garden with a central tank is adorned with flowing fountains which spray out jets of water into the air. There are small white portions which add splendour and grandeur to the fairy scene.

16. The main canal flows from the top terrace over a sloping water-fall of white marble and the water of the canals inripples flows over the carved marble into a square pond and flows on into the central tank. Between the central tank and the waterfall there has been erected the marble-throne on which Shah Jehan used to sit.

17. Shah Jehan's talented daughter Jebun-Nessa, who was a gifted renowned poetess, often sat near this waterfall with a view to listen to the pleasing rippling sounds of the water while she composed her poems. The tank at the centre of this garden is surrounded by wide brick made pavements and small pavilions where the royal ladies used to spend their happy hours in the sunshine.

18. At the north of the second terrace is a small marble tank with devices in walls for lights. This is known as the mansion of lights. Because lamps of various sizes and colours were lit and placed in the hollow spaces in the walls; while water from all the four sides to flow down past the lights, creating a fascinating fairy like scene of heavenly beauties.

19. The second terrace leads to a large garden planted with cypress and mango trees. The terrace has two water channels and tank which are decorated with row of fountains. This part of the Salimar has been drawn up in squares and is based on the favourite plan of Charbagh or four fold plot of land. The relics of the Khwabgah or sleeping room of Shah Jehan and the royal personages can still be seen in this side of the garden. The bath room lying in the east consists of four arched compartments with tanks with heating arrangements by fire on the model of the Hammam in the Red Fort at Delhi. The Khwabgah lies to the west of the garden. It is a double roomed mansion opening into a beautiful garden, planted with fruit trees and flowering sprut.

20. At the end of the garden is situated the buildings known as the "Sawan Bhadon". It was so named because the running water flowing over the marble work in the walls produced the sound exactly like that produced by rain which fall in the months of Sawan and Bhadan or July and August. These marble walls were removed by the Shikh vandals and only the trees remain.

21. Shah Jehan's court historian Abdul Hamid Lahori, the author of Badshanama better known Shah Jehannama in his history writes that the Emperor Shah Jehan himself planned and designed this garden with a view to provide a place of recreation for the ladies of the royal family so that they could enjoy themselves in privacy.

22. Shah Jehan is no more and even his Mughul Dynasty has long ceased to rule but Shah Jehan's Salimar (abode of joy) still stands out as a great monument of magnificence and splendour of the Mughul rule in India. Still if any man with least of imagination walks alone in any summer evening through this heavenly Salimar Garden, he is still charmed and bewitched with the charms and

beauties of this exquisite Mughul garden and if he has any imagination to conjure, he still hears the echoes from the dead past-the laughter of the royal children at play, the sweet voices of the royal ladies in merriment and the masterful voice of Shah Jehan calling his attendants. If he is more imaginative and pensive, he will hear the sounds of coming and going of Mughul horsemen, the voices of the Mughul soldiers, and the clatter and rattle of their weapons. The very sight of this earthly paradise rakes up and brings up to vivid memory-the transatoriesness of human power and glories. Standing at this garden one is prompted to enquire what is the true end of human power and glories, and he realises atonce the truth of the Quranic statement— "All (on this earth) fleeting and transitory and sure to fade way; only the eternal Allah and His glory everlast and shall never fade".

23.   Shah Jehan's name shall ever remain associated with the most beautiful and charming structure of the world known as "Taj Mahal", one of the seven wonders of the world, erected as token of his love for his beloved Queen Mumtaj Mahal as a memorial to his sweet memory. Though shorn much of its original beauties and glories by spoilation and ravages of time, it still stands out as glorious and magnificent monument of divine love; and still attracts millions of people to visit yearly from all over the world to admire this rare specimen of human art. Poets and writers, artists and photographers, from all countries still flock to Taj Mahal to capture and picture its picturesque beauty and charms in words and in photos.

24.   Mumtaz, a niece of Nurjahan, was a paragon of beauty and most accomplished. She was a most favourite queen of Shah Jehan. She was not only charming but also most intelligent and learned. Shah Jehan loved her more than his life and listened to her advice. They lived 14 years' happy life. When she fell ill, Shah Jehan was greatly perturbed and often remained at her bed side and often refused to take food and drink. When it became certain that she would not live, Shah Jehan with tearful eyes desired to know her last wish. The queen begged him not to forget her after death. Shah Jehan solemnly promised to remember her throughout his mortal life and erect a most exquisite and memorable monument over her tomb. Taj entombs and embodies the promise of an emperor.

25. The Taj Mahal is built of white marble with exquisite decorations and Quranic verses engraved there on. It is surrounded by beautiful garden. Inside Taj Mahal lie in eternal sleep both the lovers-the Queen Mumtaz Mahal and the Emperor Shah Jehan.

26. There are many fine stories recorded by different historians illustrative of the different phases of Shah Jehan's character. Some of these interesting anecdotes are reproduced below in brief.

27. The Viceroy of Shah Jehan at Gujrat was most tyrranical and oppressed the people under his rule. The oppressed driven to last resort throughout over a plan to bring to the notice of Shah Jehan the tyrannies of his governor and as they were affraid of the Viceroy's wrath they resorted to a device. They formed an acting party to show drama to the emperor and sent it with the merchants to the Imperial Court at Delhi.

28. The dramatic band sought permission of Shah Jehan to stage their drama and with his permission they staged a drama in which they described the oppressive acts of the governor showing the suffering and miscries of the people of Gujrat and the terrible acts of cruelties committed by the governor. This visual scene of oppression exhibited before him much moved the emperor and he cried out— "Ah, no man can be capable of such cruel acts, certainly you are depicting an imaginary scene".

The actors and merchants with all respects exclaimed— "No, it is not imaginary scene and fig of imagination, such scene is actually being enacted in Gujrat by your governor".

29. The emperor was extremely shocked at this shocking information. He ordered a court of enquiry to be held at Gujrat to enquire into the complaints made against his Viceroy. As the result of enquiries the charges were proved against the Viceroy and he was at once put into prison for trial. This shows that Shah Jehan never tolerated oppression and injustice by his officers and governors.

30. One day a person approached Shah Jehan and complained saying— "My master has not paid my wages for several months and so I am in debt to shop-keepers and cannot pay their dues."

Shah Jehan recognised the complainant to be a groom. The emperor atonce called the officer concerned and asked him if the complaint was true. The officer admitted the claim and said his salaries had not been paid through oversight.

31. The emperor made him to play the part of the groom, and when he was exhausted and tired after such acting, the emperor said to him— "You now find how hard is the duties of a groom and never fail to pay the wages of a groom who works so hard. So the holy Prophet has Said— "Pay the labourer his wages before his perspiration is dried up."

32. Once the emperor in one of his hunting expeditions was separated from his main party and tired and thirsty wanted to drink water. He found a peasant working in his field. He asked him for a cup of water and he not recognising the emperor filled a pot from a nearby well and presented it to the emperor and as the emperor was very thirsty he began to swallow water rapidly. All on a sudden the rustic peasant threw some grass in the water. The emperor was disgusted and enquired why the peasant threw grass into the water he was drinking.

33. The old frmer replied with self complacency — "That is what I do whenever I find my donkey to drink very fast. The grass makes the donkey to take water slowly so that it may not suffer from colic pain."

The emperor was not pleased with his comparison with a donkey but his innate sense of humour prevailed and he felt amused at this situation, and he was not angry at the instruction of a rustic to him as to how to drink water.

34. While after taking the water the emperor was resting his gorgeous cavalcade arrived and saluted the emperor with great respect. The old farmer was thunderstruck and fell down terrified at the feet of the emperor and begged mercy. The emperor smiled and lifted him up and said— "I am not angered, but much amused". And to show his favour to the farmer he gave him a plot of land as a free gift to him.

35. It was a custom for a royal officer to stand before the emperor and not to sit down. One day, one of his officers came to him and suddenly sat down. Shah Jehan was offended and dismissed the officer for his insolent and arrogant conduct

36. The officer smiled cheerfully and said to the emperor "I am no longer in your service. Now I can sit as free man of God as you are and I can sit at any place I like." The man's out-spokenness and courage much appealed to the emperor and he appreciated the moral courage and frank statement of the man and he saw that the man was not a mean flatterer and he is trustworthy. So he reinstated him in his former post.

37. During the time of Shah Jehan's reign a famous saint named Shah Dowla lived in Agra. The emperor wished to meet him. It so happened that one evening when the emperor and his officials were sitting on the roof of the palace, by chance one officer saw Shah Dowla walking on the street. An officer invited him to meet the emperor. He agreed. A large busket with long rope fastened to it was lowered and the saint sat on the basket and was pulled upto the roof. The emperor after exchanging usual greetings with him, began to discuss religious matters with the saint. He then said- "You are a pious and wise man, kindly explain to me what a man should do to obtain the pleasure of Allah?"

38. Shah Dowla replied— "Where there is will, there is way. Your Majesty wished to meet me, one of your ministers saw me walking on the street and Your Majesty at once lowered a busket with a rope to draw me up to the roof. Since my meeting with you, you have treated me with every courtesy and consideration. None of this was planned. The opportunity occurred and we both of us availed of it. In the same way Allah gives opportunities to His every creature to avail of His mercy and blessing in life and Allah extends His mercy to all. So that His creatures may follow His commands and earn His blessings and eternal bless."

39. The author of Lubhut Tawarrkhi Hindi (A history book of 412 pages) records— "Emperor Shah Jehan abolished the custom of prostration of the subjects before the throne. There was great prosperity in the empire during the reign of Shah Jehan. He gave

lands to the people. Notwithstanding the great area of this country, complaints were so few that only one day in a week was fixed upon for the administration of justice. Owing to the great promotion of the general wealth, and tranquility and prosperity crimes were reduced drastically". Shah Jehan's reign has been called the golden age of Indian history. His achievement in the art of building were never surpassed, not in the time of his successors; in other fields of state activity also the second. In the domain of culture his reign is marked by creative effort.

XXIV

EMPEROR   AURANGZEB

1.   Aurangzeb ascended the throne of Delhi in 1658 and reigned about 50 years. Aurangzeb had a really sound education. The half a dozen renowned scholars from whom he received education, were unable to overburden and cramp his natural gifts as has often the case with many a princely pupil. Bernier's account of his frank talk with one of his teachers is a vigorous exposition of the emperor's sound views on education.

2.   Auranzeb was the only deep scholar in his family. He led an austere life in all other aspects, but he never starved his intellect. The best portion of his intellect was devoted to his crusade against the laxities of Mughul society. He had two engagements-planning this crusade and controlling its operations and when tired refreshing himself with books.

3.   The vast range of his studies is displayed in his splendid ruqqat (letters). No topic is there that one seeks in them does not find. This collection of his letters is a unique book of wisdom and scholarship and it displays varied and vast learning and comprehensive knowledge of men and of the universe and his sound judgment and wisdom. His letters have elicited admiration and homage' from scholars even from his critics.

The other monumental work that he has left for posterity is his "Fatawa-i-Alamgiri". It is the eternal assimilation of his genius. It shows how far the emperor was alive to the basic needs of the Muslim Society of his day and in what way he endeavoured to open new channels of action for his people. His efforts at reorientation and reform eminently marks him out as the man of the hour and also as one who not only demolishes the old but also ushers in a new era.

4.   Auranzeb succeeded his father Shah Jehan as the emperor

in 1658. He did not succeed his father without struggle. He had to fight his brothers to clear his way to the throne. Aurangzeb was one of the most brilliant kings that ever adorned the throne of Delhi.

He was a pious king devoting many hours to prayers and set an inspiring example of piety for all to follow his example. Though a religious devotee, he was never unmindful of the material prosperity and well-beings of his own subjects. During his long reign essential food staffs were sold at controlled prices and the poorer classes among his subjects were exempted from taxation. Aurangzeb was gifted with exceptional abilities as a military leader and he was an intellectual giant and a great gifted scholar.

5.   Aurangzeb showed extraordinary zeal for spread of education among his subjects and ordered his provincial governors to help poor students with scholarships and stipends. He introduced compulsory primary education among the people of Guzrat, and imposed heavy punishments on truants. At Lucknow he turned a big dutch trading station into a big madrassah. Inspired by his zeal and example for education, many private persons of his time such as Gazi Rafiuddin established college. Another such college was endowed at Ahmedabad in 1697 by Maulana Akramuddin at a great cost, and a madrassah at Sialkot was liberally endowed by Moulvi Abdul Hakim.

6.   Not only the Emperor Aurangzeb was a great enthusiast for spread of education but he was a great benevolent ruler, burning with fire to make the life of his subjects comfortable and happier. From the various histories compiled to record the events of his long reign we find that during his reign the prices of grains and pulses, gee etc. in Delhi were as follows: "Wheat 20 seers per rupee; Barley 27 seers per rupee; Gram 25 seers per rupee; Sukhda rice 10 seers per rupee; Mug dal 15 seers per rupee; Mush kalai 18 seers; Mug 20 seers; Ghee 2 seers; Mustard oil 7 seers; Atta 18 seers; Red sugar 12 seers per rupee; and so on.

7.   Aurangzeb, a son of Shah Jehan and Mumtaz Mahal was the last of the first six Mughul Emperors of India. In the opinion of his father Shah Jehan his son Aurangzeb was the most qualified for the responsiblities of a great ruler. He once remarked— "The

firmness and intelligence and wisdom of Aurangzeb show that he is alone among my sons most fitted to govern India."

8.   Aurangzeb from his very boyhood was very studious in his habits and devoted his time mostly to his studies and did not waste much time in hunting and in other sports. He learned much from his talented mother Mumtaz Mahal.

9.   The emperor was much distressed at the wretched conditions of the poorer people and he also felt for those of his subjects who had no facilities to be educated.

The contemporary historians in their history books, e.g. Bokhtyar Khan in his history "Mirat-c Alam Mirat-e Jahan Numa" (who was a noble of Aurangzeb's court) gives elaborate accounts of Aurangzeb's charity and piety. The following extracts from the history "Mirat-e Alam Mirat-e Jahan Numa" is reproduced below:

10.   Emperor Aurangzeb's charity:

Emperor Aurangzeb used to distribute a large amount through sadars amongst the poor during the five months of every year. The emperor, a great whorshipper of Allah, is remarkable for his rigid attachment to religion. He says usual prayers daily in mosque and at home, and he reads the Friday prayers in the Jama Masjid with the common people. He keeps fast throughout the whole month of Ramdhan. He always refrains from prohibited food and drinks. He never put on the clothes prohibited by Islam, nor does he ever uses the vessels of gold and silver. In his court no improper conversation, no word of back-biting or falsehood is allowed. He appears twice or thrice a day in his court of audience with smiling face to dispense justice to the complainants and the aggrieved who came to his court. He hears them and dispense justice impartially. All bad characters are expelled from Delhi and throughout his empire. Under enguish and anger he never passes any order.

11.   Peace and order are strictly maintained in all the cities and towns of his extensive empire. Pensions, allowances and land have been given to the learned men and professors; stipends have been fixed for scholars according to their abilities and qualifications. All mosques of the empire are repaired at public expense. Imams and Muezzins are maintained at government expenses. He has

appointed a committee of learned jurists headed by Shaikh Nizam with liberal remuneration to compile the Fatawa-e-Alamgiri, a book on Muslim jurisprudence of eminent fame.

12. He (Aurangzeb) has ordered the remission of transit duties on all sorts of grains, cloths, other goods, and tobacco which used to bring a large sum to the government treasury as he found border officers were oppressing the people. He exempted the people from certain duties and taxes, the income from which amounted to 30 lakhs. He also abolished the practice of confiscating the estates of the deceased persons. He also issued directives to all provinces to collect taxes according to the Sharia Law.

13. Bakhtyar Khan continues— "We shall now write a few instances of his fortitude. At the time of the royal army arrived at Balkh, Abdul Aziz Khan with a large force, which equalled the swarms of locusts and ants, came and arranged his men in order of battle and surrounded the royal army. While the battle was raging furiously, the time of evening prayer arrived and Emperor Aurangzeb though strongly dissuaded by his commander alighted from his horse and said his prayer in congregation as if nothing has happened in the midst of a fierce battle. When Abdul Aziz saw this he ceased fighting saying to fight with such a man is to destroy oneself."

14. The historian further records— "The emperor is a very learned scholar and he is a hafiz. He writes elegant naskh. He has copied two copies of the holy Quran with his own hand. He has given very liberal education to the children and ladies of his families."

15. In spite of his love of learning Aurangzeb was also a daring soldier with all the dash and courage of a general. While still in his teens, he surprised the world with a blood curdling feat of bravery which shows how brave and enterprising he was even in his boyhood.

16. The Emperor Shah Jehan used to spend with his family some weeks in Agra in the winter, and during his stay at Agra various entertainment on a large scale used to be arranged. A favourite form of entertainment was a fight between the wild elephants. Once while the emperor was on such a visit at Agra it was decided to hold this favourite entertainment. A large crowd on

a vast plain gathered together to witness the wild elephants' fight, and the emperor and his ministers sat down under a silken canopy. Prince Aurangzeb and other princes rode on horse back to and from on the outer edge of the square where the fight was to take place.

17. The wild elephants brought in the battle arena and the vast crowd was on Tiptoe to see the two elephants to fight against each other. The elephants charged each other like two mighty giants but there was head on collision between the combatants. All on a sudden, one of the elephants veered round and charged straight at Prince Dara. There was panic and confusion on all sides and the people screamed with alarm and ran for life to escape the fury of the elephant. Maddened by noise the wild elephant turned to Dara with more vigour. Dara was unable to move for safety.

18. Prince Aurangzeb saw that his younger brother Dara's life was in danger. Careless of his life and safety, he at once rode his horse straight at the elephant. The elephant at once lifted him from his horse with his trunk. Aurangzeb leapt to his feet with spear in his hand and he struck the elephant with the spear to divert it from Dara. In the meantime the royal bodyguard came to their rescue and both Aurangzeb and Dara were saved.

19. Some other anecdotes reproduced from the history books of his reign throw light on the other traits of Aurangzeb's character and life conduct.

Aurangzeb was strictly scrupulous in spending money from the public treasury. He believed that a man should earn his money by his honest job. Mukhlis Khan once said to Aurangzeb— "O Emperor, Syed Sultan Mahmud is a Sayyid of the holy city of Meshad. He is living in great poverty. I request Your Majesty to grant a suitable monthly salary from the public treasury to this worthy man". The emperor considered this request and said— "I know that Sultan Mahmud has a great reputation for poetry. I also admire him. As he is not in public office, I cannot give any salary from the public money."

20. Aurangzeb, though a most powerful emperor of all India lived a life of simplicity like a common man, and always considered him to be an ordinary man, a humble creature of God. One night he called a servant to bring water for ablution to say his midnight

prayer. The servant was a little drowsy and in his haste he struck against the emperor and brought him to his knees. The servant was terrified and fell on the floor and begged for pardon. The emperor lifted him up and said in gentle tone— "Why are you so much terrified and afraid of me. I am mortal just like yourself. Don't fear me. Fear only Allah and nobody else when you disobey his laws."

21. When the emperor was about to invade the Muslim state of Bijapur, and Hyderabad, a learned judge Abdul Wahab forbade him to attack Muslim states without just cause. This advice was against the strong desire of the emperor but he showed no resentment as there was politeness or manliness in his character and he believed that every man has the God-given right to express his opinion according to his light. He continued to be on friendly terms with this judge and rewarded amply for his boldness.

22. Once an official made a special arrangement for the reception of the emperor in a mosque. The emperor was much displeased and said— "All men are equal before Allah. I am not an emperor here in this mosque of Allah. I am no more here than a meanest creature of Allah."

23. Aurangzeb with his army besieged the city of Golconda and the Mughul army was unable to force the city to surrender for long. Two Amirs of Golconda secretly accepted large sums of money from the Mughuls and treacherously opened the city gates for the entry of the Mughul forces.

24. When Amir Abdur Razzak saw this treachery, he rushed with his small band of gallant soldiers to the opened gate and attacked the Mughuls rushing to enter the city and was severely wounded. He was found lying wounded outside the city. The emperor was a chivalrous monarch and respected courage even in his enemies. When the emperor heard this, he ordered his two royal doctors to attend Abdur Razzak and he was recovered. The emperor went to see him and offered a lucrative post at his court. But the Amir replied with great respect— "O Emperor, I am greatful to you for all the kindness so generously shown to me but I cannot accept your generous offer. I am a faithful servant to my master Abdul Hasan, the ruler of Golconda. I cannot desert at this juncture of peril. The emperor was not angry but admired the Amir for his faithfulness and honesty.

25. The Emperor Aurangzeb was just and impartial to all his subjects and treated them equally. Once some leading citizen asked him to remove non-Muslims from government services. The emperor flatly refused declaring— "There is no compulsion in religion under Islam and people should not be prosecuted for their religion. The holy Quran enjoins tolerance in the matter of religion."

26. The emperor was most hard working and all devotion to duties. Once some ministers asked him not to work so hard at the cost of his health and life. The emperor calmly declared— "I live for my subjects. I have been entrusted by Allah with their well-being. A great sacred responsibility lies on my head. Do you mean I should shark this duty and leave it to others. If I do this, do you think I will remain worthy ruler of a worthy people. Allah says in the holy Quran— "Surely the best among you in the eye of Allah is one who is more careful of his duty among you."

27. Aurangzeb died at the age of ninety years and some months in 1707 A.C. He left no personal wealth behind him. He left instruction that no state money should be used for his burial, and the sum earned by him by copying Quran and sewing caps should be spent for this purpose, and should also be given to the poor.

28. Thus passed away a great emperor from this mortal world as a poor man, though rolling in wealth and power he never cared for any of them. He slept on tiger skin, and lived an austere life like a humble man. High thinking and simple living was his life motto.

29. The great and magnificent mosque known as Badshah mosque in Lahore was erected by the Emperor Aurangzeb. This grand mosque with its lofty domes and minerats visible from a distance stands as a permanent memorial to his great memory.

Though his innumerable letters are not regular history but as they disclose the inner life of a great emperor and his views, and sentiments, and his administrative ideas, his letters may be taken as historical records left by him. There are three collections of his letters-Kalamati Taiyibat, published by one of his chief secretaries-Enayatullah Khan, — the second collection under the name of Rakaimi Karaim published by a son of his another secretary, and the third has been published under the name of Dastaine Amal Aghahi. In recent times many more letters have been discovered and published. The fourth set of letters is called the Ramuz wa Isharai Alamgir. There is another set of letters called the Adabi Alamgiri.

30.   These letters and copper plates discovered to this date prove that Emperor Alamgir was not a bigotted zealot as maliciously depicted by Kafi Khan, his sworn enemy in his history and copied by other historians. He was a pious Muslim and always acted on Quranic injunctions and Prophet's precepts and guidance. He was very generous to his non-Muslim subjects and gave large grants and endowments for their temples and fixed stipends for their priests.

31.   Aurangzeb left five sons-(1) Muhammad Sultan. (2) Muhammad Moazzam Shah Alam Bahadur (well versed in Quran, tradition etc.), (3) Muhammad Azam, (4) Prince Akbar, and (5) Muhammad Khan Buksh; and five daughters -(1) Jebunnisa Begum (her learning extended to Arabic, Persian and to the various mode of writing in prose and poetry), (2) Zinnatun Nisa, (3) Badrun Nisa, (4) Zubdatun Nisa, and (5) Mehrun Nisa Begum.

32.   It is a historical fact that Muslim kings with few exceptions showed a spirit of tolerance, magnanimity of heart, broad mindedness, generosity, and spirit of service to their subjects. The Mughul Emperors of India showed such qualities eminently in India. The justice of Jehangir was proverbial. Emperor Shah Jehan was a model king and a loyal husband. His love for his Queen Mumtaz stands out unique in the marvellous monument, world-famous Taj Mahal. Even the modern most advanced architect are helpless to design a building like the Taj Mahal. The first six Mughul Emperors of India were most distinguished specimen of humanity.

33.   The Badshahi mosque, Aurangzeb's master piece is one of the most magestic mosques of the world. The great mosque is harmoniously conceived and impressively designed. It has an over-whelming majesty and grand simplicity which one may imagine carries the stamp of Aurangzeb's personality. Shah Jehan was the master-builder of his dynasty. He was one who made poems in stone.

XXV

SHAIKH AHMED OF SHIRHIND
(1564-1624)

1.   Shaikh Ahmad of Shirhind is popularly known as Mujaddid Alf-Sani, was born in 1564 A.C. at Shirhind. His father Shaikh Abdul Ahad was a direct descendant of Omar the Great. One of his ancestors Imam Rafiuddin was entrusted with the task of building the citadel town of Shirhind by Feroz Shah Tuglak.

2.   Shaikh Ahmad alias Imam Rabbani received his early education at home on theology, philosophy from his father who was a learned scholar and a Sufi. For higher education he went to Sialkot and Lahore and studied there different branches of speculative science dealing with religious matters. Moulana Yakub Kashmiri, a scholar of great repute taught him tradition or Hadith.

3.   He then went to Agra, then a capital of Akbar's empire. It was here that he came with contact with the two famous brothers, Faizi and Abul Fazl. He was also associated for some time with the preparation of that commentary of the holy Quran by Faizi which does not contain even a single dotted letter. It may be remembered that in the Arabic script only eleven letters are undotted. The wonderful feat of Shaikh of Shirhind greatly surprised Faizi who believed that Shaikh of Shirhind was the only person who can write such marvellous work in the Arabic language.

Both the brothers, though themselves great scholars had to admit the profound and vast learning of the Shaikh of Shirhind. During his stay at Agra Shaikh wrote other books on Arabic and Persian.

4.   On his way back to his home town he was married to the

daughter of Shaikh Sultan, a noble man of Thaneswar. He built a monar house and mosque with the money which his wife brought to him. He had seven sons, of whom Khawaja Muhammad Masum known as 'Urwat ul Wusqa' succeeded to the spiritual legacy of the father. He died during the reign of Emperor Aurangzeb. His brick made mausoleum lies at a short distance away from the marble domed shrine of his illustrious father.

5.   The Shaikh was a staunch believer in the maxim that there is no mockery in Islam and he had a very fine taste about dress, food etc. It is reported that on the day of his death he put on new cloths and made great preparations as if he was going on an important mission. On December 10, 1624 A.C. after the noon prayer he died and now lies in eternal sleep at a place two miles distant from the desert town of Shirhind amidst the ruins of an earlier town-the seat of the provincial governor of the Mughul Government.

6.   The shrine of the Shaikh surrounded by a stuccoed wall consists of the main sepulchral chamber, containing the graves of the saint, his wife and sons, an old mosque repaired and renovated from time to time; a meditation hall on a raised platform for visitors and votaries; residential buildings for the care takers; cubicles for foreing students and travellers; a large cemetry in which many of the kings of Afghanistan lie buried; a small orchard and the mausoleum of Khawaja Muhammad Masum, saint's second son. Every year in the month of Safar devotees and admirers of the saint gather together to celebrate the death anniversary of this leader of Islamic renaissance in India.

7.   It was Mullah Abdul Hakim of Sialkot who First proclaimed Shaikh Ahmad the reformer of the second millennium of the Hijri Era (Mujadded Alf-i-Sani). He gradually became known and number of his disciples increased.

8.   His famous epistles (Maktubat), replete with scholarly exposition of many subtle and mystic problems had attracted great notice. He was to a great extent responsible for putting a stop to the un-Islamic customs initiated by Akbar the Great, and slavishly accepted by a band of sycophants who were on the look out for

selfish gain and self-aggrandisement. His letters disclose the digraded condition of the Muslim society of Akbar's time, and he was out to reform the Muslim society of his age.

9. In one of his letters he regretfully writes— "In days goneby, the infidels being in power dominated the Muslim and openly ordered them to observe Hindu customs and religious habits. The Muslims could not practice their faith and if they attempted to do so they had to pay with their lives. What a pity! Alas! The followers of the Prophet, the chosen and the most favoured of God are humilated while the disbelievers arc honoured and exalted. Not only this the infidels jeer and gibe at them adding insult to injury."

10. In another letter he writes— "The infidels are demolishing the mosques and converting them into temples and shrines. At Thaneswar a mosque and a shrine of a Muslim saint have been razed to the ground and a large temple has replaced them both. The infidels enjoy complete freedom in the observation of their religious rites; the Muslims are incapable and helpless to the same extent. When the Hindus fast on the first of the lunar month, they take steps to see that in the cities and towns no Muslim either cooks or sells food during the day. On the other hand, to injure the religious feelings of the poor and the down trodden Muslims the Hindus openly cook and sell food during the month of Ramdhan. No one can check or prevent them because the Muslims are poor and helpless, though a Muslim King reigns over the country. It is thousand pities that in spite of the Muslim rule we the Muslims are so humbled and disgraced."

11. The Shaikh was shocked at this degrading state of things and very strongly felt the necessity of a religious revolution. The masses also longed for it. But none could dare to do that as Akbar's Government recognised no religion. Those who had the courage to tell the Muslim King that he was misled and had deviated from the true path of Islam, were reprimanded and prosecuted. The movement that grew out of the teachings and the preachings of the Shaikh was revolutionary from the start. It was a revolt against religious laxity and un-Islamic injunctions of Emperor Akbar. As the Muslim masses were smarting at the Akbar's sacrilege and un-Islamic acts,

the Muslims flocked together in large number around the Shaikh for his support but the Shaikh was against all violent revolution and Shaikh's whole mission was peaceful reform in a perfectly peaceful manner. The result of this peaceful revolution of the Shaikh was that Akbar's Din-e-Elahi and un-Islamic movement received its death knell for ever and died out.

12.   Doctor Allama Iqbal, the great poet and philosopher of the world, on the occasion of his visit to Shirhind in the East Punjab paid his homage to the great Shaikh of Shirhind in these words— "Here lies buried in this town, that great mystic, the custodian of nation's spiritual wealth, who was awakened in time by God. He did not submit to the un-Islamic demands of Emperor Jehangir and carried on his work undeterred and non-chalantly."

13.   The great historian Mullah Abdul Qadir Badauni in his famous history "Mantakhabut Twarikh" has given a graphic account of the plight which had befallen the Muslim society and the inroads which perverted ideas about Islam had made into the religious fabric under the stress of circumstances and through the inspiration which Akbar's irreligiosity had supplied.

14.   The greatness of the Shaikh lies in the fact that he reconstructed Islamic thought and was instrumental in interpreting the non-Islamic influences that had found their way into the spiritual and temporal life of the Muslims. The fundamentals of Islam had been openly attacked by Emperor Akbar and neither the classes nor the masses could resist that onslaught. It was the great Shaikh who boldly and fearlessly resisted it and successfully checked and exterminated it.

15.   During Jehangir's reign, the emperor ordered the Shaikh to come to his court, as some of his courtiers made false allegations against the writings of the Shaikh Saheb. This is apparent from the memoir of Jehangir. Jehangir writes in his memoir— "In the fourteenth year of my accession to the throne I have learnt that an imposter in Shirhind Shaikh Ahmad by name has spread his net of hypocracy and swindled for earning his livelihood. Many knaves and fools who have no scruples have been cleverly roped in. In

every city and town he has appointed his representatives who are past masters in bamboozling and mystifying the uninitiated and the ignorant. He has also prepared a book for his devotees and admirers called "Muktubat" which is nothing but clap trap and bunkum. In this book he has written at many places such stuff and nonsense which border on blasphemy and kufr."

16.   Jehangir continues— "I therefore ordered the presence of the Shaikh. He came in obedience to the royal command and his answers to the questions put by me were impertinent and irrelevant. Due to lack of intelligence and wisdom he appeared to me grossly arrogant and haughty. In order to show him his right place I ordered his imprisonment for some time. In this his mental equilibrium will be restored and the agitation against him will subside. I have committed him to the custody of the gaoler at Gwalior."

17.   For a year the Shaikh was in the jail. Earnest soul as he was, even in the prison cell his reforming missionary zeal did not abate. The Shaikh accepted his prison live as great opportunity for deeper meditation and committing the Quran to memory. He also by his life example brought about magic change in the life of the prisoners. The Muslim prisoners now began to say their prayers regularly and to perform other religious duties.

In a long letter to one Mir Muhammad Nauman, he has recounted his spiritual gains and the cultivation of the soft virtues such as humility, submission, self-efacement and resignation to the will of God.

18.   The imprisonment of the Shaikh by Jehangir was simply due to gross misunderstanding. Soon the emperor realised it and he at once ordered the release of the Shaikh. Jehangir records in his memoir— "In the fifteenth year of accession to the throne I called the Shaikh Ahmad of Shirhind whom I gaoled last year at Gwalior to my presence and set him free. I also presented him with robes and one thousand rupees for defraying expenses. He is absolutely at liberty to go where he likes and his movements are free from all restrictions. Out of mortification I told him that this act of mine was free from malice and it was meant purely for his edification."

Jehangir requested the saint to remain with the imperial army. For five years the Shaikh conducted his preaching among the forces.

19. Day and night the Shaikh preached to the forces the message of Islam, its duties and obligations. He specially preached to them the duties which enjoined upon a Muslim soldier.

The Shaikh's preaching of true Islam scorn of all un-Islamic garbage, bore fruit and Islam began to thrive again in its purity.

20. The Shaikh did immense service to the noble cause of Islam in India and his zehad against the emperor's un'Islamic campaign was eminently successful and knocked out the life out of this irreligious heresy.

21. As a result of the Shaikh's exposition of sufism, the whole system of sufism was harmonised with the Islamic thinking as interpreted by the companions of the holy Prophet.

The confused thinking of certain sufis influenced by the Hindu system of philosophy was now purged of all dregs and dross and un-Islamic ideas and the Indian sufis were brought back into the true path of Islamic thinking. The Shaikh well-deserves the title of an Mujaddid.

XXVI

SHAH WALI-ALLAH

1. Shah Wali Allah was the most celebrated traditionist, jurist, sufi, and scholastic philosopher. He stands out an outstanding figure among the great thinkers and scholars who have made a thorough study of the evolution of human society through the ages. His findings on the evolution of the human society are most original and excellent, and most modern. The theories propounded by him have been accepted by the world as the approved postulates.

2. Shah Wali Allah though a great mystic did not believe in asceticism or renunciation of the world for the sake of spiritual achievement. He was rather of opinion that if all the people of the earth give up the world and were living ascetic life in caves and lonely places for attaining spiritual perfection, the world would become a desert and the human race would become extinct. According to him this course is not he will of Allah. According to Shah Wali Allah man's spiritual progress is co-ordinated with social and economic progress. Man's daily engagements have their due effect on the soul. They either darken it or enable it to receive the blessing of divine knowledge as the case may be.

3. For this reason, he says, prophethood also includes in its programme the removal of economic inequality from among the people. For example in the time of the holy Prophet Muhammad, the ruling calsses of the two great empires-the Roman and the Persian-had become so lavishly luxurious in their habits that the working people were virtually reduced to the position of beasts of burden and the holy Prophet was commanded by Allah to end this inequal economic condition.

4. After the death of Emperor Aurangzeb, the glory of the

Mughul Empire was gone and the empire greatly declined the Muslims of the empire received a rude shock and shattering blow. Political decadence went hand in hand with moral, social and economic degradation. In the midst of this ever darkening gloom, only one enlightened Muslim held out the torch of light. That family was the family of Shah Wali Allah. Among his family members Shah Wali Allah is the greatest of all.

5.   Shah Abdur Rahim, the father of Shah Wali Allah was born in 1640 in a family with great military tradition. But Shah Abdur Rahim took an academic life. He received his early education at Agra from Muja Zahid in religious literature. Shah Abdur Rahim taught in the Madrassa-i-Rahimyah until he died in 1717 at the age of seventy-seven.

6.   Shah Wali Allah was born in 1703 during the reign of Emperor Aurangzeb. In his early life he showed signs of his future greatness. His learned father taught him first. At the age of five years he went to school. He committed the Quran to memory and became a Hafiz-i-Quran within two years and he began to say daily prayers and to keep fast at the age of seven. He was a wonderful genius and highly meritorious. By the age of ten he completed the study of all important works on theology and received instructions on medicine, mathematics and rhetoric as well.

7.   After his father's death he began his career as a teacher for some years but meantime he twice went on pilgrimage to Mecca and stayed there in Arabia to complete his studies under Shaikh Abu Tahir of Medina, a great scholar of his time.

He came back in 1731 to Delhi and began his programme of giving speeches, delivering sermons and composing books on different branches of Islamic literature. He died in 1762. Before he died he had laid the foundation of a revolutionary movement known in history by the name of "Hibzi Wali Ullah (the party of Wali Ullah). This was a central organization with a net work of branches spread over the whole sub-continent. This organization played a great role in the Muslim revival.

8.   Shah Wali Allah's greatest service to the revival of Muslim power in this sub-continent is the translation of the holy Quran into persian in the teeth of vehement opposition by the orthodox of his time. But he did it and declared boldly— "The importance of the Quran lies more in its teaching than in its beauty in literature and perfection in style." In his teachings Shah Wali Allah emphasized the importance of Tauhid (unity of God), but in its interpretation he did not go to the extreme and he was not intolerant towards those who differed from him. He was not a bigot or narrow-minded. He went back to the past of inspiration.

9.   Shah Wali Allah was a true Mujtahid and resorted to Ijtihad. He protested against undue veneration shown to some saints. He kept balance between the temporal and spiritual spheres of life and in such balance of mind lies his greatness.

10.   Shah Wali Allah has not written any separate book on social evolution. But in all his important books such as— "Hujjat", "Al-Badrul Bazigah", "Al-Khairul Kathir", "Tafhimat" etc. He has elaborately dealt with the growth and evolution of human society in different ages, and the causes affecting its progress and disintegration.

11.   Shah Wali Allah's theory of social evolution is most interesting. A synopsis of the same is given below:

According to Shah Wali Allah the origin of the entire universe is the same and there is a central organization governing the movements of every thing existant. The creator has assigned a fixed sphere of activity for each one of them which is in complete harmony with the activities of others. If any goes wrong any where in the world of matter, the worlds of soul and simplitude (Alami Ruh Alam Mithal) are moved to action at God's command and the defective part is eliminated. The divine will is that human beings should move steadily toward perfection; God therefore inspires some intellectuals with some noble ideas capable of discovering things and inventing means to maintain such a progress towards perfection.

12. Shah Wali Allah classifies this evolutionary process of human society into four distinct stages:—

(1) society of the dwellers of the hills and forests,

(2) society of the villages inhabited by tribes,

(3) urban society or civilized group,

(4) international society.

The life of the people living in forests and hills is much similar to the beasts; because they are less concerned with social obligations.

The rural society is a stage higher than the former; because in it an individual understands a little his obligations to a particular group brought together by common sentiments.

The society of the dwellers of the towns forms still higher a stage of development in which man's civic sense becomes more perfected, and daily life more regulated.

But the highest of all is the stage of internationalism wherein the common brotherhood transcends the limits of clans, tribes and nations. But such a stage is not always possible; because the fittest individual (or a group of individuals) is available but only once in many centuries.

13. According to Shah Wali, a primitive man has a family, a form of speech and a co-operative link with other such families.

14. About rural stages he says— "This rural stage extends over a larger group of people living in the plains and engaged in various occupations. They respect the word of the person or persons whom they have accepted as their leader and follow his or their advice in all matters. In this stage, life in the general sense has become more co-operative and co-ordinated, and the leaders have great responsibility to fulfil.

The children should be educated according to their personal aptitude and the future needs of the community. It is the duty of the leader to see that every one is provided with work.

SHAH WALI'S VIEW ABOUT LAND

15. Land which produces staple food for the community must not be given permanently to a selected few. The land should belong to the cultivators, each one having as much as it is possible for him to till with convenience. The cultivator should be allowed to reclaim more soil from the marshy or other areas provided it does not interfere with the rights of any one. The mines and woods should by no means be given over to any particular person.

Poverty is bad, because it affects the character of man.

16. About the town and national stage Shah Wali's views are most modern. He says— "Leadership of the town must under all circumstances be in the hands of a real person or persons. The leader should be a model for all others. The best thing is that his election should be unanimous. Otherwise the dissenters will always create troubles."

17. According to Shah Wali Allah religion is an integral part of society. The primary purpose of every religion is to introduce among the people four important qualities *viz*, moderation, humility, purity and generosity. These qualities strengthen the general morale of society and provide it with unity of action and spirit.

18. Shah Wali Allah's exposition of the stage of internationalism:

To avert mutual fueds and wars, bloodshed between states, an international system of government is indispensable. Such a system is possible only among those nations who have a common religion and the same standard of culture and civilization. The continuity of such a state is possible if the system of government by which it is run is very sound. The head of the state whom Shah Wali calls the Caliph (Khalifah) must be capable enough to handle all situations which may arise from time to time. He should know his duties in war and peace, be impartial in his judgment and promt in his decision.

19. Shah Wali Allah had four sons-(1) Shah Abdul Aziz (born in 1746), (2) Shah Rafiuddin (born in 1749), (3) Shah Abdul Qadir

(born in 1753), and (4) Shah Abdul Gani. Of his sons Shah Abdul Aziz was most known.

Shah Wali gave a fatwa against the oppressive rule of the British and wanted a religious war to be declared against them. But Shah Abdul Aziz supported the study of the English language. The Delhi College had rejected the fatwa of his father and he believed that time had not come to fight against the British and also believed that it was necessary to fight against the Sikhs first. In the religious war that was carried against the Sikhs, his pupil Sayyid Ahmad of Bareilly and his own nephew Shah Ismail (son of Abdul Gani) took a leading part and died as martyres at Balakot in 1831.

The greatest contemporary of Shah Wali Allah was Muhammad Bin Abdul Wahab, who was the founder of the Wahabi movement.

An estimate of Shah Wali Allah:-

Shah Wali Allah Dehlvi was the greatest advocate and the pioneer of the Islamic revival movement in India. He was a prolific writer and a great thinker whose works are famous for richness of thought and vigour of spirit. His books are an source of inspiration. To those who are interested in the political, religious and cultural history of Islam. Shah Wali Allah was a religious psychologist, the philosopher of history, sociology and political science. He was also an educational thinkers, whose contribution to the theory and practice of education in India was great. According to him Din (Faith) is a vast term, it includes secular activity also; in his opinion, education is nothing separate from Din. Because all education is for Din, and Din in its essence is nothing but perfect life in both worlds. Shah Wali Allah revised the curriculum in the light of current political requirements.

XXVII

TIPPU SULTAN

1.   Sultan Fateh Ali, well-known as Tippu Sultan, was an illustrious son of a worthy father, Sultan Haider Ali, the founder and architect of the kingdom of Mysore. The lion hearted Sultan Tippu came off a martial race. His father Sultan Haider Ali began his life career as an ordinary soldier, but being gifted by extraordinary virtues and daring, rose to the throne of Mysore by his own achievements. Mysore always remained a Hindu kingdom. It was Haider Ali who made it a Muslim kingdom.

2.   Sultan Tippu was born in December 1751. Sultan Tippu grew up to be a stout personality. He acquired all the great virtues and talents of a great soldier and of a great statesman from his great father under whose able and wise guidance he was brought up. He was well-educated and was well-versed in literature. He was an expert horseman and an excellent swordsman. He was a man of spotless character, matchless courage and of firm determination. He had unbounded zeal and extraordinary vigour and dashness. He was an eloquent orator, fluent speaker and masterful writer. He was admired and praised for his undaunted courage and bravery. He was greatly honoured for his great foresight and wisdom. Allah gifted Tippu with great administrative ability and great political acumen and sagacity.

3.   It is reproted that from the age of six to the death of his father Tippu always went with his father in all the battles. And thus he learnt in practical field the art of war fare and its tactics. He was placed in the command of selected soldiers when he was sixteen years' of age. At this young age he had to face the English army at Bangalore and he gave a crushing defeat to the English.

4.   After his father's death, when he ascended the throne of

Mysore he had to fight valiantly against three powerful enemies-
the English, the Marhattas, and the Nizam of Hyderabad, and
against a powerful combination of these three. He was a great
fighter and would have succeeded in defeating them and driving the
English from India, had not the treachery, conspiracy, and mean
perfidy on the part of some of his own people, and the base plotting
and perfidious role of his relatives had not stood in his way. He
suffered much by such vile acts and had to sacrifice his precious
life for the freedom of India. With him ended the last hope of
India's deliverance from foreign rule.

5.   Tippu was a great invaluable asset to the Muslims of
India-nay to the whole of the Islamic world. Tippu Sultan was an
ardent champion of liberty and freedom and greatly resented the
domination of any foreign country over any Islamic state and Asia.
His motto and golden maxim in life was "The Lion's one days' life
was better than that of Jackal's hundred years' life". In that his
was the once powerful voice raised against foreign subjection and
exploitation. He was a true Muslim to the core. He harboured a
burning desire to unite all the Muslims of the neighbouring countries
to smash and destroy the nefarious designs and evil intention and
the plotting and plans of the foreign imperialists' powers, such as
the English, the French to dominate Asiatic countries.

6.   Sultan Tippu was a most foresighted statesman of his age.
He clearly foresaw the coming danger of foreign subjection of Asia
and Africa and to avert it and to take timely steps to check it he sent
his best Emissaries to Turkey, Egypt, Persia, Afghanistan inviting
them to unite together for a common cause namely to combat and
prevent the foreign subjection of Asia and Africa.

7.   He discerned well in time that the storm of Western
subjugation and exploitation was coming and if it is not resisted in
time by an united, all co-ordinated forces of all the Muslim
countries the result would be fatal and the Muslim Asia and Africa
would soon fall prey to Western domination and subjection and
would suffer bitter sufferance, but Tippu's lonely warning was not
heeded to. Even the Nizam of Hyderabad was beguiled into the trap
of the British and allied with them to crush Tippu. The Marhattas

also allied with the English against Tippu Sultan. The British diplomacy won the day.

8.   The fearless lion hearted Tippu only remained unbending and resolute and fought to the last to hold out the torch of liberty to the East. The indomitable national hero Tippu Sultan continued the war against the combined forces and carried on a ceaseless struggle against the English for the liberation of the Indian subcontinent and fought single handed. He captured Bednore and Mangalore and forced the English at Fort St. George to sign the Treaty of Mangalore in 1784 whereby the English recognised the Sultan's right to certain districts claimed by the Nizam.

9.   The English under Lord Corn Wallis, violated this treaty and formed a triple alliance with the Nizam and the Marhattas against Tippu. Tippu had to begin again his struggle against English and their allies which ended with his gallant martyrdom on the battle field in 1799 A.C. The martyrdom of Tippu removed the last stronghold of independent Muslim power on the subcontinent and the whole India lay prostrate before the British might. On hearing the news of the death of Tippu Sultan, the British Governor General Lord Corn Wallis declared with extreme joy— "Now the British dominion in India was so safe and secure and the only rising danger to it has been removed by the death of Sultan Tippu."

10.   The noble character of Sultan Tippu and his very generous treatment of Hindus have been distored and falsely written and misrepresented by his enemies. He has been represented as a Muslim zealot who forcibly spread Islam among the Hindus. It is a damned lie and perversion of truth.

11.   In this twentieth century most modern scientific civilized world, in spite of loud talks and full-mouthed slogans and declarations, the weak and the minorities are unable to get their full citizenship rights and freedom as for example— *"In secular India the Muslim and Schedule castes minorities are not getting their equal rights and freedom with Caste Hindus"*, even in the U.S.A. Negroes are not being treated as equal citizen. Still segration, ghettos, apartheism prevail in South Africa, South America, and other places.

12. If we compare the freedom of conscience, religion, free worship, political, social, and economic equal rights given by Sultan Tippu to his non-Muslim subjects with that of the treatment of the modern democratic governments to their minorities and backward subjects, it well be clear as day light that the treatment meted out to Hindus by Tippu was more generous, more humane, and more just and equitable.

13. Tippu was a pious Muslim well-versed in The Quran and traditions and he knew of the Quranic injunction, "there is no compulsion in religion", and also the holy Prophet's precept to treat non-Muslims generously.

The noble-minded Sultan never attempted to convert any non-Muslim to Islam by force and he never maltreated the Hindus. Now documentary evidence is available to prove that the pious Sultan treated the Hindus very humanely and generously. The letters written by Tippu in 1791 to a Hindu Guru (preacher) of Seringri and pecuniary aid rendered to him, coupled with grant of land, clearly testifies to his magnanimity of heart and nobility of soul.

14. Tippu was most just and impartial. It happened that one of his own sons took away some vegetables from the field of a poor cultivator. When a complaint was made to him, he was angry and awarded severe punishment to his son.

On another occassion when a trusted counsellor of the Sultan asked to dismiss a certain Brahmin official, he refused to do so declaring— "The holy Quran orders that only those should be punished who treated others highhandedly and unjustly". Such a pious God-fearing Muslim Sultan cannot treat non-Muslims unjustly. He has been purposely and falsely depicted as a tyrant and hater of Hindus.

This vicious allegation against the Sultan is positively disproved by a historical fact that "the Sultan ordered his army not to throw any bomb of any kind on that part of the port Dundigall where the Hindu Raja had built a temple though the military strategy and demand required the bombardment of that part of the fort. The Sultan looked to the religious sentiment of his subjects more than to military advantage".

15. Sultan's reforming activities:

Prior to the reign of Sultan Tippu the women of southern India used to be dressed half-naked. They wore a dhoti (loin cloth) to cover the lower parts of the bodies, leaving the upper parts including breasts uncovered. The Sultan ordered all women to wear shirts, headresses and pyjamas. Still women are seen in the same half-nakedness in Southern India where the influence of Sultan's reform have not extended.

He abolished many immoral customs and polyandry, devadassies (temple dancing girls) and other evil usage among the Hindus.

16. The Sultan opened schools for the untouchable. Jagirs were granted to the temples and Brahmins. Scholarships and stipends to all irrespective of caste and creed.

17. Tippu Sultan was a remarkable personality. He was God-fearing and pious, just and tolerant and benevolent ruler. He respected the Islamic laws and never broke the injunctions of Islam. He not only showed kindness to his Muslim subjects but also showed large hearted generosity to his non-Muslim subjects. He administered justice impartially to all high and low.

An estimate of Sultan Tippu:

When a detailed history of Indo-Pakistan's freedom struggle comes to be written a place of very high distinction will be found for Sultan who stood up against the British and fought and died in the battle field, thus symbolizing the very best in the valiant band to India's freedom fighters. Tippu Sultan fought against alliens not for his dominion but for freedom of India. Tippu was not only a great champion of the then India's independence but he was the first martyre for the noble cause of national freedom. He was a great enlightened monarch of Asia.

L.B. Bowring in his book Haider Ali and Tippu Sultan mentions that Tippu's library contained a respectable collection of manuscripts mainly on religion, philosophy, theology, sufism, ethics, poetry, history and jurisprudence.

◆◆◆◆◆

XXVIII

SAYYID AHMED SHAHEED BARELVI

1. The most pernicious and baneful affect of a foreign domination and subjection on a subject people is that it creates in the ruled a servile mentality and moral degradation. Sayyid Ahmed Shaheed was in fact the first who started the first movement for the establishment of independent homeland for the Muslims and who gave his life in the battlefield for free Muslim India.

2. Shah Abdul Aziz, worthy son of Shah Wali Allah organised the great renaissance movement under the name of Targhib-i-Muhammadia to purge the Muslim society of un-Islamic and evil practices and to infuse the true Islamic spirit into the minds of the Muslims. This movement was organised on All-India basis and composed of selfless workers. This movement soon developed into a movement of liberation of the Muslims from the foreign subjection of the Shikhs and the British. The men chiefly responsible for this freedom movement were Ismail Shaheed of Delhi nephew of Shah Abdul Aziz and his guide, and master Sayyid Ahmed Shaheed of Rai Bareli who himself was a disciple of Shah Abdul Aziz.

3. Sayyid Ahmed Shaheed was of a Sayyid family whose great ancestor had settled down on the outskirts of Rai Bareli during the reign of Emperor Aurangzeb. The boy Ahmed Shaheed paid little attention to his books to the great despair of his father. He would roam about in the country side or on the banks of the Saye Stream with other boys of his own age, enjoying such vigorous outdoor games as kabbadi, and wrestling, swimming, and riding. If sports was a passion with him, social service was acraze with him. He enjoyed nothing so much as doing little chores and humble services to the poor country-folk.

4.   Sayyid Ahmed continued to exercise vigorously his moral and physical powers by engaging in work of social service and social welfare and physical exertions till the age of 17 years. At the age of 17 years he had a strong noble personality with little learning. When he was seventeen, his father died and two or three years after his father's death young Ahmed left for Lucknow with a party of friends to seek employment and to see the world. He found a patron in the noble disciple of his father but the monotonous luxurious life of Lucknow made him disgusted, he soon started back to Delhi and after a tedious journey on foot, he came to Shah Abdul Aziz.

5.   The disarming simplicity, the frank and dignified bearing and earnest look of 20 years Sayyid Ahmed made a profound impression on Shah Abdul Aziz, who placed him incharge of Shah Abdul Qadir, the great scholar and pioneer and the first translator of the Quran in Urdu. Sayyid Ahmed was now taught in Shah Abdul Qadir's Great School at Akbari Masjid. He soon proved himself a veritable God-gifted genius and excelled others in his knowledge and intellectual attainments.

6.   Thereafter he returned to Bareli in 1808 and married Zohra Bibi. Then he returned to Delhi but soon left for Tonk in Central India where he took up military service with the Nawab Amir Khan to learn the art of warfare. Nawab Amir Khan was fighting against the English and was playing an important role on the chess board of that troubled times.

7.   Sayyid Ahmed was imbued with a spirit of selfless service to Islam. He therefore attached himself to the Nawab as an active warrior and was soon honoured not only with important commands but with the confidence and respect of the Nawab who always sought his advice. He served the Nawab for six years but when he found that the Nawab taking huge money from the English and making alliance with them to attack Madhopur, he tried to dissuade the Nawab not to ally with the English and not to take their money, but he found him too weak, and greedy, he left his service and came to Delhi with the young prince entrusted to his care.

8.   The third visit to Delhi in May 1818 was a new era in his life. He was now fully equipped for spiritual guidance and took his abode in the Akbari Masjid. The fame of his spiritual greatness spread far and wide and the people in thousands visited him for guidance. Shah Ismail and Abdul Hye became his disciples. Henceforth his whole life was devoted to supreme efforts to bring about regeneration of Islam in India.

9.   In 1819 Sayyid Ahmed visited Ghaziabad, Saidam, Meerat, Muzaffar Nagar, Shaharanpur, and Deoband to preach his life's mission. Whereover he went, he brought about regeneration in man's life by his preaching and his own example of life. During his tours he first heard about the bitter prosecution of the Punjab Muslims by the Shikhs and he felt profound sympathy for his oppressed Punjab Muslims.

10.   Sayyid Ahmed's Teachings:

The special feature of Sayyid Ahmed's teaching was the elimination of Sham and Humbug from religion and the adoption of the simple and sincere ways of the Prophet's life in all walks of life. While in principle his insistence was on a strictly unitarian conception of God with the consequent eradication of all "Shirks" such as the adoration of saints and shrines, in matters of practice his preoccupation was the spread of sunna or adherence to the ways of the Prophet. He emphasized on the importance of godly living so that every act of human life may be actuated by a noble intention, seeking the pleasure of Allah only. His general message to all was "Live a pure simple life on the true Islamic pattern."

11.   Sayyid Ahmed went on pilgrimage to Mecca with many of his disciples and he stayed in Hedjaj for fourteen months. On his return from Mecca to India Sayyid Saheb started a campaign to collect men and money for sending expedition against the Shikhs. He sent out letters to the religious leaders of the country, urging them to consider Jehad as an important principle of Islam and to help in its prosecution.

12.   In his letter to Nawab Suleman Jan he wrote—

"Unfortunately for some years India has come under the rule of Christians and Hindus, and they have started prosecution and oppression in a large scale on the Muslims and Islam being suppressed. This has deeply touched my heart and yearning for Jehad has awakened in me."

13. Sayyid Ahmed realised and again and again proclaimed that political power and sovereignty was essential for the regeneration of the Muslims society. So having completed all necessary preparations, he wanted to make the Frontier provinces his headquarters because he needed the help of the warlike Frontier tribes in his Jehad. For this purpose he left his home town of Bareli in 1826 to spend his life in waging active war in the way of Allah and for independence of Islam, and to liberate the Punjab Muslims from the opperssive subjection of the Shikhs.

14. He appealed for men and money to all Muslims of all parts of India. Funds poured in from far and wide. Arms, equipments and horses kept coming in. Thousands of Muslim warriors flocked to his banners. When the first expedition left, it composed of 12,000 Mujahid army and many thousands followed later on. The Nawab of Tonk who was a most devoted disciple of Sayyid Ahmed invited him to visit Tonk where necessary arrangements, preparations for the campaign were finalised with the help of the Nawab. The long and tedious journey from Bareli to Tonk, then across the desert of Sind, then through Hyderabad and Shikarpur over the Bolan Pass to Kandahar in Afghanistan took many months and caused much hardship. Ultimately it reached Nowshera.

15. From Nowshera proclamation was issued inviting the Shikhs to either accept allegiance or war. The Shiksh failing to do either; a night attack was made on Shikhs by 900 Mujahideens on the whole Sikh army with such conspicuous success that the whole frontier ranged with praises of their bravery. The several tribal sardars especially Yusuf Zais joined Sayyid Saheb.

16. A Shikh army of 30,000 came to exact tribute from Muhammad Khan and his brothers of Peshwar. Khavi Khan persuaded the Shikh army to help him to regain Manpari. But when

the Mujahideens came to defend Manpari the Shikh army after several skirmishes fled away.

17. This signal success against the Shikhs impressed the people greatly and ten thousand warlike men from Garhi Imazi under Sarwar Khan accepted Sayyid Saheb as sardar, and the people of Peshwar invited him to organise a war against the Shikhs.

A huge army of one lakh men under Sayyid's banner collected but the Sardars of the Peshwar were won over by the Shikh general Budh Singh. They arranged to poison Sayyid Saheb at the battle of Shaidu but Sayyid Saheb managed to survive miraculously due to strong vomitting and went on a battle on an elephant. As the Sardars of Peshwar all went over treacherously in the battlefield and joined with the Shikhs and thereby disheartened the Mujahideens so much that they lost the day.

18. After this great setback due to sheer treachery, Sayyid Saheb with his Mujahideens had to face three enemies-the Shikhs, the Sardars of Peshwar, and Khavi Khan of Hund. But undeterred and undaunted the great Mujahid Sayyid toured the Frontier regions visiting the courts of Nabira and Swat. From his letter to the Nawab of Tonk it appears that during his tour he was able to gather three lakhs under his leadership.

19. The Mujahideen camp presented a unique spectacle. In this vast camp every one helped mutually and were imbued with the highest morale and the religious ideals. They were inspired with a new life and new ideal of life. The whole campaign was supplied and sustained by a vast net work of the Targheeb-i-Muhammadia organisation in India, headed by Moulana Ishaque and Moulana Yakub grandsons of Shah Abdul Aziz. Caravans continued coming continually with men, money and supplies. All money and materials received from India and also the booty were kept in the Baitalmal under the supervision of Moulana Muhammad Yusuf who distributed the same so justly that even Sayyid only received his own share.

The rulers of Punjtar, Fateh Khan and Ashrab Khan, in whose territory the headquarters of the Mujahid army was located helped Sayyid Saheb in all possible ways. In this vast camp every one was a model of self-help and performed religious duties regularly and every one was eager for service and self sacrifice. In spite of many discomforts the camp looked very much like a holiday camp, so gaily and cheerfully did every one go about his business. Courtesy and social graces no less than moral values and religious exercises were never lost sight of Shah Ismail used to explain the Quran daily.

20. During all these times clashes and skirmishes with the Shikhs continued. The Sardars of Peshwar now openly allied with he Shikhs. They continued to despatch expeditions after expeditions against the Mujahids but these expeditions were always repulsed. To make the matter worse, not only Khavi Khan but also the local population was incited by him to fight the Mujahideens.

21. Sayyid Saheb decided to deal with Khavi Khan first and he sent a small force under Shah Ismail to take Khavi Khan and to capture his fort. Ismail cleverly defeated Khavi who was killed in the battle and captured his fort. Khavi Khan's brother came with a large force but he was defeated at the battle of Haryana by the Mujahid army. Yar Muhammad brother of Khavi Khan was killed. Now only the Shikhs and Sultan Muhammad of Peshawar remained to be dealt with.

22. Now the headquarters of the Mujahid forces were shifted to Kashmir. Ranjit sent a peace mission and behind it an army led by a French General and Sher Singh. No peace was made. Durranis allied with the Shikhs but their combined forces were defeated by the Mujahid army. After this great victory Sayyid Saheb had no difficulty in marching into Peshawar. He was received with great enthusiasm everywhere. Now he achieved his mission to a large extent and he now restored Islamic rule in a large area. From Amb to Mardan his dominion was recognised.

23. But still the octupus of treachery spread its tantacles to scotch the healthy Islamic life enforced by Sayyid Saheb.

Sultan Muhammad sought forgiveness. Sayyid Saheb out of his innate goodness forgave him and Sultan Muhammad solemnly swore and undertook to govern according to the law of Islam. Moulana S. Mazhar Ali was appointed a Kazi in his state. Sayyid had no personal ambition but was only the desire to see the government according to the injunctions of Islam.

Numerous workers worked day and night with missionary zeal to reform the Muslim society but unfortunately their honest zeal and intention against the entertia and deep-rooted prejudices or the local people roused resentment. Their lost morals, evil practices and barbarous way had the sanction of local custom and a superstitious creed. So when the reformers assailed these, they antagonised both the local people as they withheld them from unIslamic self-indulgence and the priestly class and pirs as they deprived them of the power that ignorance and superstition gave them so a violent reaction followed and treacherous Sultan Muhammad treacherously took advantage of this, murdered all reformers one night in Peshawar and in all his territories.

24. This great calamity came as a great blow to Sayyid's noble mission. At one stroke he lost some of the noblest workers among his followers and a large and important territory and he also lost the hopes of establishing the Islamic society of his dreams. He decided to leave Frontier regions and to go to Kashmir as he found to his bitter disappointment that all his teachings and efforts to bring the people to the true path of Allah had gone in vain.

25. In his letter dated 13th Ziqaad 1236 or 1831 from Balakote to Nawab Vizir-ul Daula express his feelings thus:

"Since the people of the plain of Peshawar were accursed unfortunately, they did not choose to join the Mujahideen in this Jehad but rather succumbed to the seductions of the infidels and murdered a number of our leading spirits who were scattered over the countryside for various reasons. The main army remained safe and ready for the service of God but as our sole object of staying there was to secure the support of a large body of the Muslims to crusade against the infidels and as this can no longer be hoped for, we have decided to move from there into the hills of Pakhh. The people of this place have received us with open arms and promised solemnly to join in the Jehad and provided us land to live in. So I am peacefully encamped in Balakote which is one of the passes in this district, and the army of the infidels is too encamped three or four miles away from us. We are secure but the Mujahideens plan to give battle in two or three days. I have every hope that Allah would help to win victory then Inshallah all the country upto Jhelum and all Kashmir will come under our sway. Please pray for the advancement of Islam and success of the Mujahideens."

26. In the great battle of Balakote again treachery played its fatal role. Of the two ways that led upto Balakote in those days, one had become overgrown by the jungle and was almost unknown except to a few local people, while the second passed through a narrow defile and over a bridge where the enemy could be held easily but some treacherous miscreants betrayed secret of the jungle path to the Shikhs. The Shikh forces poured in from this path and spread out. A grim battle took place the at Balakote in which the great Mujahid Sayyid Saheb with his glorious band of Mujahideen slost their lives and attained martyredom in the way of Allah in 1832.

27. Thus ended the noble life of the greatest noble Mujahid for a free Islamic state in then sub-continent that Islam produced, so cruelly betrayed.

Sayyid Ahmed Shaheed did not die in vain. The noble cause for which he gave his life blood triumphed and his puritanical movement survived and was carried on by his disciple Moulana Kerat Ullah Jaunpur who vigorously carried it on among the Muslims of Bengal and Bihar.

28. Sayyid Ahmed Saheb stood up against un-Islamic superstition and malpractices. He also championed the cause of Muslim sovereignty. More than a century after the Muslims of India on 14th August 1947 won their sovereign home land free from foreign subjection to mould their lives according to the injunctions of Islam and precepts of the Prophet.

29. In the Annals of Indian history the Mujahideen movement was the first popular movement against alien rule. It was a popular

movement which was started, fostered and maintained for over
half a century by the people. It was also the first Islamic movement
in India which had for its raison de'tre Islam-nothing but Islam. It
for the first time emphasized that the Indian Muslim was a distinct
and separate political, social, religious unit in India. Even such
hostile critics as W.W. Hunter has characterised this movement as
one of the greatest religious revival that has ever taken place. The
Mujahideen raised the banner of Islam from the dust, held it aloft
for more than half a century with varying degrees of success and
founded an Islamic republic, though for a short time. This move
was first directed against the Shikhs and when the Punjab was
annexed by the British, it was turned against them.

30.   The fire kindled by the freedom and reform movement did
not go out with the martyredom of Sayyid Ahmed Shaheed. In
1831 his disciple Titu Mir in Bengal led an infuriated peasants
rising against the oppression of the Hindu landlords created by
Lord Corn Wallis of the Judigo Planters and other oppressive
agencies. Titu Mir became strong enough to hold supreme sway
over the whole of the country north, and east of Calcutta including
the three districts of 24 Parganas, Nadia and Faridpur, to defy the
British civil and military authorities, beat back several expeditions
sent to destroy him, to proclaim the cessation of the British rule and
the re-establishment of the Muslim rule. All this took place within
a couple of hours ride from Calcutta.

31.   The British had to send a fully armed artillery division
against Titu Mir, who, with his followers entrenched themselves in
his bamboo camp. Titu Mir died fighting for the freedom of his
country.

Bevan Jones in his book "The People of the Mosque" Says—
"The movement survived him (Sayyid Ahmed) mainly because he
had infused in his followers a passion for a free home land and a
reformed Islam."

Some of Sayyid's followers established a camp at Sittahana.
Moulvi Velayet Ali and Inayet Ali successors of Sayyid Ahmed
covered the entire country, either in person, or through their

Emissaries, and established provincial, district and local centre to collect money and recruits to call people back to puritanical Islam and call on them to contribute for the Mujahideen camp at Sittahanah and such was the people's response to their stirring appeal that even in southern India the women cast their jewels in the common purse and on the other hand company after company of recruits were sent from all over India, especially from Bengal; and they covered their long treck on foot to the Frontier.

32. Mr. Hunter says that the Mujahideen forces kept British from 1830 to 1857 so much engaged that the English had to send sixteen expeditions of 33,000 regular force against them. By 1863 the British were forced to send 20 separate expeditions aggregating 60,000 regular troops beside irregular auxiliaries and the police. Though Sittahana camp was destroyed with 5,000 Mujahids but the movement continued and the British failed to crush the movement. In the Ambala campaign the British were worsted and according to Hunter "left the fatal defile (the Ambala Pass) thickly planted with the graves of the British soldiers and their casualties were immense over 900. The British suffered in the 42 expeditions between 1849 and 1890 sent against the Mujahideens."

33. The Mujahideen movement, though weakened remained undaunted as ever and master-minded and made another coalition, took the offensive and faced in 1868 a formidable British force on the Black Monutain. But even this formidable British campaign failed as the Punjab Government admitted in its letters— "Come to a close without our having been able to drive out the Hindustani fanatics to their homes". The Mujahideen movement including its literatures had mentally prepared the Muslims to make a supreme effort of oust the British from India. This was the first freedom among the Muslims which resulted in the establishment of Pakistan.

XXIX

MOULANA JALALUDDIN RUMI

1.   Moulana Jalaluddin Rumi, one of the greatest poets was born at Balkh in Khurrasan in 604 A.H. 1207 A.C. 30th September. His father Bahauddin Sultan Walad was known Sultan-ul Ulema for his great learning; and his mother Mumine Khatun was the daughter of the Amir of Balkh. His family claimed descent from the first Caliph Hazrat Abu Bakr. When three years of age, his father took him to aged Attar at Nishapur who foretold the future greatness of Maulana Rumi. His father Bahauddin had to leave Balkh as incurred the displeasure of Muhammad Kutubuddin Khwarizmshah.

2.   His father with young Jalaluddin went to Erzincan, stopping on the way at Baghdad, Mecca, Medina, Damascus, Aleppo and Malatya. During his long migration Bahauddin Walad found the opportunity to meet the important personalities of that age. Later from Erjincan he went to Kayseri, Sivas and Nigde and arrived in Karaman in 1221 A.C. where he stayed for seven years and the Amir of Karaman, Musa, started a madrassah for his teaching and his son Rumi married Gawar Khatun from Samarra.

3.   Moulana Rumi's father ultimately settled in Konya. At that time Konya was the capital of Seljuki Turkish Sultans and a great centre of science and art. The then Seljuki Sultan Alauddin Kaikobad invited Sultan Walad and his family to Konya. Rumi's father died at Konya in 1231 A.C. After his father's death Moulana Rumi received important instructions and education from well-known scholars of that age, such as Burhanuddin Tirmizi, Serajuddin Armevi and Sadruddin Konevi, when Moulana went to Damascus and Aleppo for his education he also came there in contact with great Islamic scholar Muhuyuddin Arabi and learnt sufism from

him. On his return to Konya his name and fame spread far and wide and he had many hundred students in the college of Konya. At this time he was given the title of Moulana Rumi by the Europeans. Seljuk Sultan Kaikobad appointed him a professor.

4.   Since then he never left Konya but for a short time. The even which had the greatest effect on his intellectual and moral life was his meeting with the Sufi Muhammad Shamsuddin Tibrizi who came to Konya on a visit. He saw Jalaluddin and he exercised greatest influence on him. Rumi acknowledged what he owed to his master Shamsuddin by dedicating a great part of his work to him. As a result of this meeting he gave up studies of science and the profession of teaching and entirely devoted himself to sufism. When Shamsuddin suddenly disappeared from Konya Moulana Rumi was much perturbed and in his great sorrow for Shamsuddin wrote his Divani Kabir. He wrote his great work Masnavi by the encouragement of Hussamuddin Chelebi.

5.   Moulana Rumi suddenly fell ill and his illness lasted for forty days. The whole population of Konya, men, women and children, the Saljuk Emperor Ghyasuddin Kaykhusrav III came to visit him. But all efforts for his recovery failed and Moulana Rumi died on 17th December 1273 A.C. All people without distinction of race or creed attended his funeral to pay their last tribute to Rumi.

6.   Moulana Jalaluddin Rumi was a poet of the first rank. He possessed the most diverse qualities, variety and originality of imagery, dignity and picturesqueness, learning and familiar charm, deapth of feeling and of thought. As a philosopher he is less original than as a poet. His teaching is that of Sufism, expressed with glowing enthusiasm.

7.   Moulana's Ideals:

The Moulana was principally a mystic poet. His mission in life was to love and respect mankind. He was utmost tolerant. Goodness and charity were the distinguished characteristics of his noble character. All throughout his life he lived a life full of genuine love. His love was the love for Allah. His main works are based on the love of Allah. "In the presence of Allah every body is equal. Every person who knows how to repent for his sins has won the right to live and the person who knows to love always deserves to be loved"-are some of his prominent sayings. His another prominent saying is "Useless striving is better than slumbering". God is the most active being and loves activity. Every day he is busy with some thing new. The sovereign ruling the universe cannot sit idle. He loves movement; therefore "a useless effort is better than utter passivity".

8.   Rumi is a preeminently mystic but he has nothing with quietism, generally associated with mysticism. He was a practical thinker, above all a man of action. Rumi has strongly asserted the individuality of man and says that man does not lose his individuality when he acquires divine attributes as an iron does not cease to exist as such even when it becomes red not in fire and acquires the property of fire.

Rumi holds that man has been endowed with free will since he bears moral responsibility for his actions. Although human will is subordinate to divine will, yet it cannot be said that divine will stands in the way of man's freedom of choice. According to Rumi human actions proceed from choice and are never predetermined but their consequence, of course, are predetermined, that is, they follow from the law which rules the universe and every individual being. This law of life Rumi says is the Taqdir or destiny and this law is no doubt immutable and it is in quite fitness of things that such a law should be fixed and unalterable for otherwise there will be no order, harmony or discipline in the administration of the universe.

9.   To Rumi proof for the existence of free human will lie in the act that when a man commits a sin or a wrongful act, he repents for it afterwards. This repentance, Rumi says, would not be felt by him, if he were not possessed of free will.

Rumi regards love as the soul of universe and to Rumi love is the food of all lives and the cure of all ills. He further says that love is the astrolabe in which divine mysteries are revealed.

According to Rumi the status of perfect man is not reserved for the aristocracy but on the contrary it is open to all.

10. Rumi's Ethics :

Moulana Rumi's ethics is essentially directional. It is absolutely subjective and essentially personal. As he says— "Trust thy heart if thou art upright. Remember it if thou art free." Morality, he emphasizes can never be objective. Morality coming as it is, from the essentially free choice of man can never be same thing as given, nor can it be codified. It is the peculiar concern of heart rather than of mind. The free morality of the free individual is thus peculiarly their own. Accordingly conscience, if it is based on feeling is a dangerous guide. In moral progress love alone can direct man in moral yearning. Rumi's conception of morality is thus not the morality of the traditional school of thought. It is the doctrine of universal love preached universally.

11. Moulana Rumi's Work :

Moulana Rumi was a younger contemporary of Ibnul Arabi, the great Andalusian formulator of mystic principles. Jalaluddin Rumi was great a scholar in theology and philosophy, and at the suggestion of his friend and disciple Husain-Uddin he composed his celebrated work-the Masnavi. This work is one of the greatest mystic poems of the world and in oriental thought it stands high. It contains about 27,000 verses in which a complete teaching of sufisim is narrated and illustrated by means of anecdotes, fables, legends etc. quoted from tradition and from passages taken from the Quran. The Masnavi has a very lucid and perspicuous style. It gives the reader an exhilarating sense of largeness and freedom. The Masnavi tells us that the greatest virtue is ishk or love, which helps in purification and attaining a vision of the supreme being.

Religious rituals and prayers are good. The essential object is self-purification through faith and God is pleased with love and sincerity rather than with the observance of the religious code and rituals.

12. Rumi was an out and out evolutionary thinker. His other works are:-

(1) The Devani Kabir-consisting of 21 volumes of 96,000 couplets of love and mysticism.

(2) The Fih-i-Mufih-is a didactic work and contains the sermons and dictations of the Moulana.

(3) The Majalisi Sabha—is in Arabic and consist of his seven pieces of advice.

(4) The Muktubat-is a collection of his 1444 letters written by him to the important men of his time.

13. Moulana's Mausoleum :

At present Moulana's Mausoleum is the Konya Museum of antiquities. His tomb is the monastery founded by him. The architecture of this 'Tekke' is of remarkable delicacy and beauty; the mosque is adorned with carved candelabra, valuable tapestries, embroideries and beautifully engraved inscriptions.

XXX

DJAMAL UDDIN AFGHANI

1.   Djamal Al Din Al Afghani, Al-Saiyed Muhammad Bin Safdar was one of the most remarkable figures in the Muslim world in the ninteenth century. He was, according to E.G. Browne, at once philosopher, author, orator and journalist; but above all a politician regarded by his opponents as dangerous agitator. He exercised great influence on the liberationists and constitutional movements which have arisen in the Muslim countries in the last two decades.

2.   Jamaiuddin agitated for their liberation from European influence and exploitation, for their independent internal development by the introduction, of liberal institutions for the union of all the Islamic States including Persia under a single caliphate and the creation of a powerful Muslim empire capable of resisting European interventions. Jamal-Al Din was one of the most convinced champions of the Pan-Islamic ideas with tongue and pen.

3.   The present twentieth century is witnessing a wide-spread Islamic Renaissance. The Muslim States which once were under Western or other foreign subjection have become or are becoming independent sovereign Muslim States. Islam and Muslims are awake every where. A great reawakening is visible in every nook and corner of the Muslim world. A spirit of revival, revivification and regeneration is pulsating the Muslim heart every where. The world of Islam is humming and stirring with vigour and activity. One great son of Islam who has contributed much to this revival and liberation of the Muslim world was Syed Jamaluddin Afghani.

4.   Sayid Jamal-Al Din was one of the prominent leaders of the Muslim revival movement. Through ceaseless efforts he awakened

the Muslims from their deep slumber and inertia, lethergy and coma, and placed them on the board path of self-help and self-reliance. He raised his powerful voice and wielded facile pen against the imperialist foreign exploitation or subjection of the Muslim people. He inspired in the Muslims the indomitable spirit to live again as man and to revive and restore their past glories and glorious living.

5.   Allama Afghani had a dynamic personality and possessed a sterling character. He was an intellectual giant of high calibre, a foresighted statesman of powerful personality. In fact he was a versatile genius. Allama's family traced it descent through the famous traditionist, Ali Al Tirmidhi from Hussain bin Ali which entitled them to hold the title of Saiyid.

6.   According to Syed Afghani's own account, he was born at As'adabad near Kanar in the district of Kabul in Afghanistan in 1254 A.H. 1838 A.C. in a Hanafi family. According to others he was born in Asadabad in Persia but in order to escape Persian despotism he claimed Afghan citizenship. In any case he spent boyhood and youth in Afghanistan. Syed Safdar, his father, was a celebrated Alim of Afghanistan and was well—known social reformer and he educated his son in the best possible way and young Jamaluddin finished his education in Quran, Hadith, Tasawwaf, Law, Philosophy, Chemistry, Medicine, and all other higher branches of learning till his eighteenth year, at the same time devoting attention to the study of philosophy and exact sciences.

7.   After the completion of his studies he went in pilgrimage to Mecca and on his way to Mecca he stayed in India for one year in 1856 and contacted all important leaders. It so happened that the first great war for the liberation of India took place in 1856. On his return from Hedjaj he went to Afghanistan and entered the service of Amir Dost Muhammad, but after the death of Dost Muhammad owing to succession disputes, he had to leave Afghanistan.

8.   He visited many Muslim countries and he was shocked at the degraded condition of the Muslim world. He found the Muslim world as a house divided against itself and he also noticed that

every Muslim country was a hot bed of intrigues, feuds and conspiracies. The great soul of Allama was much aggrieved at the sorry and sad state of affairs. He gave his choicest thoughts to the problems of the Muslim world and planned out a feasible scheme to bring about revival and reawakening in the Muslim world about their glorious past and of their glorious future.

9. In Afghanistan Allama took on himself the task of the education of the Crown Prince Muhammad Azam and tried to infuse in his mind his ideal and ideas of the revival of the Muslim world. When Muhammad Azam became the Amir of Kabul, he appointed him as his Prime Minister but he had to leave Kabul owing to family feuds. He then went to Cairo and stayed there for a short period. He came in contact with the Azhar circles and held private lectures and also at Azhar and organised a group of youthful workers including his disciples Abduh and Zuglool. The Egyptian Monarch scented danger in his activities. So Allama had to leave Egypt.

10. By this time his reputation and fame spread far and wide and he was invited to Turkey.

He was given a heroe's welcome in Turkey. He was soon appointed to the council of education and invited to deliver public lectures in the Aya Sofia and the Ahmedia mosque. A lecture delivered for students by him in the Dar-ul Fanun before a distinguished gathering on the value of arts in which he mentioned the gifts of prophecy among the various social activities gave offence to Hasan Fahmi, the Shaikh-ul Islam, who was jealous of Allama's growing influence and gave an opportunity to charge him with revolutionary views, owing to mean intrigues of his opponents he had to make up his mind to leave Constantinople and to go to Cairo where he was very kindly received by the authorities and the educated classes.

11. The Egyptian Government granted him an annual allowance of 12,000 Egyptian piastres without any definite official duties. He was free to instruct the young men who assembled round him at his house. He gave them lessons in his free discussion on the higher branches of philosophy and theology and at the same time pointed

out to them the way to literary activity. In politics also he influenced those around him in the direction of the Islamic revival and liberal Islamic constitutions; his activities exercised influences on the nationalist movement which came to a head in 1882 and led to the bombardment of Alexandria, the battle of Tell-e-Kabir and the English occupation.

12. A little before this in 1879, Allama whose political activities were inconvenient to the English representatives as his regeneration of philosophical studies had been irritating to conservative ulemas of the Azhar, was at the instigation of the English deported and detained in Hyderabad in India and later in Calcutta until after the suppression of the Arabis rising he was allowed to leave India.

13. During the period of his detention in Hyderabad he composed his refutation of materialism.

From India Allama went to America and stayed there for some months. In 1883 he visited London for a short period and after this with his devoted friend and disciple Mufti Muhammad Abduh who was in Paris; where he began his propaganda and literary activities. He strongly protested against the British intervention in the affairs of the Muslim people. The most prominent and influencial newspapers lent their columns to his essays, to which much attention was paid by competent authorities on the oriental policy of Russia and England, conditions in Turkey and Egypt, the meaning of Mahdi movement which was started in Sudan.

14. During this period also his polemic with Earnest Renan arising out of the latter's Sarfarne lactures on Islam and science, in which he stated that Islam did not favour scientific activities, was composed by Allama. Jamal-ad-Din which sought to refute this in an article which first appeared in the journal Des Debates also in German Papers.

The quarter part of Allama's literary activities were devoted to an Arabic newspaper published at the expense of a number of Indian Muslims with the help of Mufti Muhammad Abduh, called Al-urwat Al-uthka which unsparingly criticised British policy in

Muslim countries. The first number of this paper appeared in March 1884, and was suppressed by the English authorities and its entry to Egypt and India was banned. This paper exercised great influence in the awakening of the liberationist anti-British views in the Muslim world and can be styled the first literary harbinger of the nationalist movement in the Muslim territories of England. Even to this day copies of this paper is popular in all Muslim countries.

15. In 1886 Allama received a telegraphic invitation to visit the court of Shah Nasiruddin in Teheran where he was given a most distinguished reception and was shown great honour and he was given high political offices. But this did not last long, because the Shah soon becoming suspicious became weary of his increasing influence and growing popularity. So Allama had to leave Persia under pretent of ill health. From Persia he went to Russia where he again entered into important negotiations and remained till on the occasion of his visit to the Paris exhibition of 1889. He met the Shah who was then in Europe and was induced by him to accompany him to Persia. During his second visit to Persia, Allama felt more vividly the fickleness of a ruler's favour. He enjoyed full favour and confidence of the Shah for some time but the intrigues of his Grand Vazier Ali Mirja Ali Asghar Khan who was jealous of the Allama's learning and popularity resulted in creating mistrust of the Shah to which the Allama's proposed reform of the administration of justice contributed much.

16. Recognising the danger of his position he took shelter in the sanctuary of Shah Abd-Al Azimnear Teheran which was considered inviolate. Allam stayed here for seven months surrounded by a body of admirers who listened to his discourse and views on the reforms of down trodden countries. But in 1891 the Shah instigated by his Grand Vazier, quite regardless of the inviolability of the sanctuary arrested the Allama with the help of 500 cavalry and brought him in extreme winter in chains to the Turko-Persian border Town of Khanekin. After a brief stay in Basrah Allama went again in England and from there carried a campaign against the oppressive rule of the Shah in Persia by letters and otherwise. Tobacco concession granted to a foreign English company presented

a God-sent opportunity to the Allama to rouse the popular feelings against the Shah and his Grand Vazier Ali Asghar. It produced a terrible effect. The Persian Ulemas a powerful body issued a fatwa to Persian people not to use tobacco so long this concession remained. The reform movement in Persia acquired a great momentum and the Shah of Persia was murdered in 1896.

17. During his second stay in England Allama was more active politically. He received through the Turkish Ambassadar Rustam Pasha in London Abdul Hamid's written invitation to settle permanently in Constantinople as the Sultan's guest. He accepted the Sultan's offer reluctantly. Besides a monthly allowance of 35 Turkish pound, a beautiful building on the Nishantash Hill near the imperial Yildiz Palace was given to him where he was able to live in comfort and meet people who sought his inspiring conversation.

Here Allama spent last five years of his life between the Sultan's favour and disfavour. But here also he was a victim of court intrigues and sought the Sultan's permission to leave Turkey, but always, the permission was refused. According to a German visitor Allama was in a kind of gilded cage.

18. Allama Jamaluddin died on the 9th March 1897 of a cancer which began in his chin. It is said that his death was due to poison administered to him by Dr. Abdul Huda, a dangerous opponent of Allama at Abdul Hamid's court.

19. Allama Jamaluddin Afghani had immense love for Islam and the Muslims. His whole life was devoted to the service of Islam and the Muslims. He spent a life of a brisk revolutionary activities. He was a sincere soul so sincere that every word that flew from his mouth sparkled with the glow of his deep sincerity and sober thinking. He analysed the cause of the Muslim decline and came to a finding that the cause of the Muslim decline lay in their disunity and internal feuds and dissensions. He was an arch enemy of imperialism, colonialism and imperial exploitation; and tried level best to awaken the Muslim world to the dangers of colonialism and foreign exploitation. He was a firm believer in Islamic democracy and intended to set up a Shurai Nizam.

20. Allama wrote very little in spite of his scholarly command of Muslim theology and philosophy. His treatise against materialistic philosophy, that is, Dahriya which appeared in three languages is important. He wrote a short sketch of Afghan history under the name of Tatimmat-Al-Bayan. His activities were mainly to publishing inspiring political articles. In addition to Al-Urwat-Al-Uthka, he was joint founder and an industrious contributor to the bi-langual (Arabic-English) monthly "Diya-Al-Khafikaini (splendour of the Hemisphere).

21. Allama stood for freedom, liberty, equality and Pan Islamism. The aim of his life mission was proclaimed in his weekly Al-Urwat-Al-Uthka. These aims were:

(1) To organise the Muslim countries into one organic whole and to cultivate in them the belief that the Western powers are taking advantage of their internal disunity, dissension, mutual jealousies, and rivalries and are exploiting them for their Imperialistic designs.

(2) To set up a system of collective security in the Muslim world so that if any one Muslim country is attacked all the member countries would employ their full resources to defeat the aggressor collectively and unitedly.

(3) To encourage other Asian countries, to revolt against the yoke of imperialism and to attain freedom.

22. Allama Jamaluddin's greatest service was that he awakened the Muslims from their deep slumber and age long inertia and frustration and instilled and infused in them a spirit of freedom and strife and created in them an urge to revive the past glory of Islam. It was he who organised the reform movements in Turkey, Iran, Egypt, Afghanistan and in many other countries. He inaugurated a new era of freedom and liberty in the Muslim world. From him flowed a regeneration in the Muslim world culminating in the creation of Pakistan and the establishment of the independent Muslim state of the present world. His Pan-Islamic movement was a master stroke of policy. In order to liberate Turkey and other Muslim countries from foreign yoke he decried all distinctions

of cast and creed or colour and emphasized on the basis of the essential unity of the different sects of Islam. He wanted the Sultan of Turkey to, be the Khalifa of the Muslim world.

23. Allama was a true son of Islam, the great inspiring message which he gave while dying to the Islamic world is an unique document and an eloquent testimony of his intense love of Islam and of the Muslim. He said with his dying breath : "Now I am in such a state that I neither need the tiding of death nor the hope of life. Neither am I afraid of death nor grieved over my imprisonment. I am happy over this imprisonment, for my body is in prison for the cause of freedom of the Muslims. I am being assassinated but I am happy over this death, for I am giving my life to give life to my Muslim nation. My oppressors are unaware of the fact that death of one who stands for a noble mission is never the death of the mission itself. Nay, because of it rather the words of truth becomes imperishable. Now I would let you know my last desire : "Gird up your lions for the heroic fight for freedom. Never be afraid of trial or tribulation arrest or assassination. Never bow before odds. Never worry over the sly artifices of the Kings and Monarchs. Carry on the fight with firm conviction and robust determination. Nature is with you, and Almighty Allah is supporting you. The upsurge of freedom is moving at a heavy pace. It is going to sweep away the cob-webs of the entire east and fill it with life as water fill the ocean. Go ahead, I wish you God-speed."

This glowing and soul stirring words of Allama Jamaluddin sent a thrill and stirring throughout the Muslim world and moved the Muslims to a new urge, a new spirit, to a new life and to a new era of independence and liberty. Allama lived and worked and died not in vain.

XXXI

HAFIZ OF SHIRAZ

1.   Hafiz of Shiraz was the famous Persian lyrist and one of the most outstanding poets of Persia. He has been given the title of "Lisan-ul Gyab (the tongue of the unseen) by his admirers. He is also called "Turjumanul Asrar (the interpreter of mysteries).

2.   The grandfather of Hafiz migrated from Ispahan to Shiraz during the reign of Atbeks of Shiraz. His father Bahauddin was a rich   merchant but he died untimely leaving three sons who squandered the wealth left by him. Hafiz was the youngest among his brothers and he lived with his mother. Due to poverty Hafiz was forced to work in a baker's shop.

3.   Hafiz had a love for learning. Whatever time he could scratch off from his work in the baker's shop he spent in his studies. Out of what he earned he gave one-third to his mother, the other one-third paid to his teacher and the remaining one-third to the poor and the needy. Hafiz was a persevering and hard working student, soon he acquired a good education and learnt Quran by heart, for which he adopted his pen name or lakh as Hafiz.

4.   During this period a spirit of poetry and romance was in the air. There was a cloth merchant in the locality who was a great admirer of poets. There in his shop gathered from the different areas of the city every evening many poets and recited their poems. This assemblage of poets gave an opportunity to Hafiz to compose his poems also but with little success; on the contrary the people made fun of him. Being bitterly frustrated and disappointed, one night he wept bitterly and prayed to Allah for his success as a poet. It is reported that in that night he saw in dream Hazrat Ali who gave some thing to eat and assured him that henceforth the gate of

poetry as well as knowledge were opened upon him. The following morning when he work up he composed a poem which was of great poetic beauty and all were greatly surprised by newly composed poem. Nothing succeeds so much as success. This success encouraged him. He began to compose lyrics in Persian and his fame as a great lyrist soon reached far and wide.

Hafiz now received invitations from the royal houses of India, Iran and Arabia to visit their countries, but as he was so much bewitched with charm of Shiraz, he was not prepared to leave it, event for a time. His poem and couplets are full of high praises of the rose gardens, charming scenes and pleasant climate of Shiraz.

5.   Moulana Shibli Nomani in his famous work "Sherul Azam" (the poetry of east), have mentioned the names of several rulers whose favour and patronage Hafiz enjoyed. One of this was Shaikh Abu Ishaq Inju, a semi independent ruler of Shiraz. Himself a reputed poet Abu Ishaq was a great patron of arts and learning. Hafiz saw several rulers of Shiraz who succeeded one another. All were impressed by the poetic genius of Hafiz and all favoured him highly.

6.   It was during the time of ruler Zainul Abdin that Taimur Lang (Taimur) visited the city. Doulat Shah, in his famous book "Tazkaratul Aulia" has recorded in detail this historic meeting of these two outstanding figures of the age—one the greatest conqueror of the world, and the other the greatest poet of that time. On his arrival in Shiraz Timur Lang who had conquered a great part of the then world sent for Hafiz Shirazi and confronted him with this verse— "If my beloved could conquer my heart I would bestow Samarkand and Bukhara for her mole"— "have you composed this couplet" asked the Taimur Lang. "Yes"— replied Hafiz. "Do you know, I have run over the entire world in order to build up Samarkand and Bukhara which are my native place and you are prepared to give them away in return of a mole only"-enquired the awe-inspiring majestic Taimur Lang.

7.   Hafiz remained unmoved and unperturbed and replied— "This is on account of such extravagances that I have been reduced

to this state of poverty". The great emperor in whose presence the mighty rulers trembled with fear was much amused with the retort of Hafiz and rewarded him with presents and wealth.

8. Sultan Ahmed Ibn Owais-i Jalair, the talented Ilkhani ruler of Bagdad invited Hafiz to visit Bagdad. He replied in verse— "The Zephye-breeze of Musalla and the stream of Ruknabad do not permit me to travel or wander afield."

9. Two of the Indian kings tried their best of induce Hafiz to see their courts. One of them was Muhammad Shah Bahamani, a great patron of art and culture. He even sent the travelling expenses and a ship to take Hafiz to his court. He sent his man with money and presents to escort the poet from Shiraz to Gulbarga. Hafiz spent a considerable part of this money in Shiraz and on his arrival at the Persian Gulf he gave the remainder of the money to a destitude friend. Two Persian merchants bound for India offered to bear his entire travelling expense. When they reached Hurmuz a ship was waiting to convey the poet to India but when the ship was about to set sail a hurricane blew and Hafiz landed ashore from the ship. He, without going, sent the following few couplets on the occasion to King Mahmud:

"Not all the sum of earthly happiness,
Is worth the bowed head of a monent's pain;
And if I sell my Dervish dress,
Worth more than what I see is what I gain.
The Sultan's Crown with priceless jewels set,
Encircles fear of death and constant dread;
It is head dress much desired and yet,
Art sure' tis worth the danger to the head?
Down in the quarter where they sell red wine,
My holy carpet scarce would fetch a cup;
How brave a pledge of piety is mine,
Which is not worth a goblet foaming up!
Full easy seemed the sorrow of the sea,
Lightened by hope of gain hope flew too fast;
A hundred pears were poor indemnity
Not worth the blast."

10. Another Indian King Sultan Ghyasuddin of Bengal invited Hafiz to visit his court, but the poet did not accept his invitation and sent him an ode. Hafiz had a good knowledge of Arabic language which is proved by his bilingual poems.

11. Hafiz is universally recognised as matchless in the realm of lyric. His successors including poets Saib, Urfi, Salim have acknowledged his incomparable skill in lyric. Hafiz not only expanded the scope of Persian lyric through his epicurian philosophy which was earlier expanded by Omar Khyyam in his quatrains, but he immortalised Persian lyric through his inimitable style, his sincerity and sublimity of though and richness of experssion.

12. Before the advent of Hafiz, Saadi and Khusrus had beautified Persian by the lyric in simple diction. Salman Sawaji and Khwajoo Kirmani made Persian lyric attractive and enriched it with linguistic ormentation and flourish of rhetoric. Hafiz was a devotee of Shiraz and he is never weary of singing the praise of Ruknabad and the rose garden of Musalla. He sings of spring rose Nightingale wine youth and beauty.

13. According to Sir Gore Onsaley, Hafiz's style is clear, unaffected and harmonious displaying at the same time great learnings and matured sciences and intimate knowledge of the hidden as well as the apparent nature of things; but above all a certain fascination of expression unequalled by any other poet.

14. Miss Gertrude Lowthian has made the following estimate of Hafiz:

"To Hafiz on the contrary, modern instances have no value. Contemporary history is too small to occupy his thought—but some of us will feel that the apparent indifference of Hafiz (to his environment) lends to his philosophy a quality which Dante does not possess. The Italian is bound down within the limits of his philosophy, his theory of universe is essentially of his own age and what to him was acutely real is to many of us merely a beautiful or terrible image. The picture that Hafiz draws represents a wider landscape, though the immediate foreground may not be so distinct. It is as if his mental eye, endowed with wonderful acuteness of vision had penetrated into these province of thought, which, of later age were destined to inhabit. We can forgive him for leaving for us so instinct a representation of his own time and of the life of individual in it."

15. The poetry of Hafiz has a universal appeal. Hafiz is undoubtedly one of the most popular poets of the east. The poems of Hafiz 693 in number have been translated into several Western languages—English, German, French, and Latin.

16. Hafiz died in 793 A.H. and was buried in a green orchard in the suburbs of Shiraz which was later called after him as Hafeziyya. His tomb was built by Abdul Qasim Baber, the great grandson of Timur Lang and subsequently beautified by later rulers. It is now a place of recreation and pilgrimage for the visitors drawn from distant countries. The poets words came out to be true:

"When thou passest by our tomb seek a blessing, for it shall become a place of pilgrimage for the lebertines of all the world."

17. The Divan of Hafiz is one of the seven poetic wonders of the world. Hafiz was one of the many people who combined a religious life with the writing of the poetry.

The world's love and sorrow have depicted by Hafiz thus:

"Openly I declare and am glad of my declaration,— I am the fountain of love and am (therefore) free from Shaikhs of both the worlds."

"I am a bird from the holy garden. How shall (or can) describe the hardships of my separation."

XXXII

GHALIB

1. Ghalib, one of the greatest Urdu poets of Indo-Pakistan sub-continent was born on 27th December 1797 at Agra, the home of Taj, and died in 1869 A.C. Ghalib spent few years of boyhood with his mother at the house of his father who was a commandant in the army at Meerat. His father was a notable citizen of Agra. While he was five years of age he was deprived of his parental affection. His uncle Nasarullah Beg who was a Risaldar in the British army and was married into a rich family of Delhi undertook to rear up Ghalib.

2. When Nasarullah visited Delhi he took young Ghalib to Delhi. Ghalib was of seven years of age. Ghalib's misfortune was not over. His dear uncle Nasarullah all on a sudden died leaving Ghalib to toss to and fro in the sea of miseries. It is said that the school of adversity is the man's best ground for developing character and development of genius. Ghalib from his boyhood received his training in the school of adversity and developed his poetic genius in that school. He goes on to say that the reward for each act of a person follows immediately according to its nature. If a man does a good act, the mental pleasure that accrues from it is an ample reward; if a person does an evil act, the retribution is the painful feeling of guilt. That is he thinks of heaven and hell to be, but a state of the mind. Now if a person is helpless in doing what seems to be good or evil, why he is given promises of heaven and threats of hell? Ghalib, like Ibn Taimiyyah (died 1328 A.C.) believes that both these are here in this world, So Ghalib sings:

"Sev'n times more painful than hell
Is shame that follows evil deed
Thinkest thou not that it is
For the criminal ample need?"

3. Ghalib believes that whatever the state of a man's mind might be, he is found to be in sorrow and affliction as long as he lives in this unreal world and does not realise his own true identity or self. The path of man's deliverance is above the cool shades of heaven and the raging flames of hell. It is above the Ka'bah and the Cathedral, which are in a way a veil between a man and the reality.

"The path of man's deliverance is the stair way of love", that leads his union with the absolute, just as the salvation of a drop of water lies in its mingling with the vast ocean.

4. Ghalib married early at the age of 13 years into the same family of Delhi as his uncle was married. Ghalib's married life was most unhappy. In one of his letters he refers to his unhappy marriage in a charming allegorical way in these words: "Thirteen years since my birth I spent in prison (the world) and then I was sentenced to life imprisonment. A fetter was put around my feet and the city of Delhi was the gaol into which I was thrust. His childhood as well as youth was full of distress. Even his afternoon that is the old age was not free from a fresh tides of tragedies against which he could no longer fight with the patient and courage of his youth. All of his seven children died prematurely to his great shock and when the wound of their separation was still green in his heart, his adopted son Arif whom he loved very much for his tender speech and presence of mind died a young man. This tragic incident upset Ghalib for some time and he wrote such a pathetic elegy in Urdu, that a reading of it can not but brings tears to eyes, that have never been moistened before.

5. In 1857 when a fierce revolution for the deliverance of India from the British domination was in full swing, Ghalib's life also underwent a revolution, his monthly stipend from the Red Fort (the Mughul Emperor's Court) ceased because of his connection with Bahadur Shah Zafar (D. 1862 A.C.) and the pension which he received from the British Government was also suspended on suspicion. It was restored three years later when he was found to be guiltless. With his pecuniary crisis came another sad tragic incident. Ghalib's only younger brother Mirza Yusuf Khan whom he held dearer than his life died at the age of 24 in the prime of his

youth. Ghalib never forgot this sorrowful even and often refers it in his poems and letters.

6.   Ghalib was a great philanthrophist and in spite of his financial stringency he paid liberally to the poor and the needy. During three years in which his pension was suspended he passed through acute monetary crisis, he had to sell or mortgage his household articles to meet his necessary expenses. He sings of these days thus:

"Days when rain gladdened the earth and nights when the moon lit the sky; — where dark in my eyes.

Many a Spring found me searching for the necessaries of life, Many a time the world has been gay with the rose and the tulip While I have been living moodily in my cell Indescribeable is that Which passed on Ghalib's head This disdained creature had no God Is it all that can be said."

7.   Ghalib as a Poet:

In the necessary qualification of an artist Ghalib shines more dazzlingly than other poets, copying faithfully what he sees and experience that makes him outstanding figure in the galaxy of poets. Ghalib does not stoop to write flattering verses in praise of the wealthy men to win their favour, even his old age and chill penury did not force him to do so. Ghalib relies more upon nature, who winks at him to use his special faculty of observation to extract the essence of daily experience hidden from the human eyes. Ghalib was an imitator of nature and more than, that, he was as an instrument of nature. Ghalib himself says:

"Were verses the order of the day Thy name would to the pleiades shine And, Ghalib, had it religion been Thine would be the book divine."

Ghalib says— "Book divine" because the ideas flow into the poets's mind from above. As Carlyle very aptly says— "He speaks with the voice of a God". For this reason in Arabic poets are called the pupils of God.

Ghalib composed 1883 couplets in Urdu. There are in his poetry frank realisation of human nature, there are palpable truths about this world and the next world, there is humour with cynicism, pathos, ethics and philosophy.

8.   Ghalib's Philosophy:

It is specially to be noted that though Ghalib never studied the treatises of Western philosophers, yet most of his philosophical ideas conform to Western philosophers' theories.

Ghalib believes that in the begining there was nothing but God, then prompted by the desire to see what he was like, he cast his reflection on the great void. Ghalib expresses his belief thus:

"Lord, was it not to see thy beauty

That thou gave the power of sight."

The great Muslim philosopher of Spain Mohiyuddin Ibn Al Arabi (D. 1240 A.C.) was of the same opinion of Ghalib.

9.   Ghalib also believes like great philosopher Schopenhaner that this world, the reflection of God's image, is unreal and exists in the mind. He says: "The world an empty name I find — all matter figment of mind". It was Omar Khayyam who first profounded this theory.

It appears from a trend in his poetry that Ghalib believes like the famous philosopher Descartes — "Cogito, ergo sum", "I think, therefore I am". But according to Ghalib, the human ego is like a drop out of the ocean, only infinitisimal part of the eternal reality. It is not reality itself. To the discerning eye the very presence of our existence is a proof of a super-conscious existence, just as it sees in a drop of water, the presence of an ocean. He says:

"Not to see in a drop the Tigris

And the whole by part supplied,

Is not to have the seeing eye

But the playing of a child."

10.   Ghalib from his very infancy was brought up in the most adverse circumstances. The pathos of sorrows and happiness which runs throughout the whole gamut of his poetry is due to his life of miseries. If he had not suffered these turmoils, tribulations, ups and downs in life, his poems would have been devoid of all those sad and sublime thoughts—would have been too without half the sweetness. As it is said that sweetest songs are those that tell of saddest thought. Though Ghalib had no regular proper schooling but before him was the open book of nature, the greatest teacher of all times (so greatly enjoined by the Quran) and the best of guides. Nature taught him when to smile and when to weep, and blended in his nature a proportionate amount of humour and pathos that is reflected in his poems. In his Urdu and Persian poems there are verses to amuse and infuse bright hopes into saddened hearts. He says:

"All our dreary hopelessness

Is in time forgot

Before the joy of struggling on

E'en tho'result is nought."

11.   Asadullah Khan Ghalib died on 15th February 1869; and now lies buried in Delhi in a poor mans grave of which Ghalib has himself sung thus:

"A watery bier I'd fain embrace—

No funeral march, no resting place

To suffer after death disgrace."

Shakespeare was not recognised in his life time. But Ghalib was recognised as a great poet and it is irony of fate that his grave is neglected

12.   It recalls to memory the poet Hasan's Couplet, ah, if there ever shall arise a nation whose people have forgotten poetry or

whose poets have forgotten the people, though they send their ships round Taprobane and their armies across the hills of Hindustan, though they mine a league into the earth or mount the stars on wings—what of them Hasan: they shall be dark path on the world.

13. The great national poet or Iqbal has compared the poet Ghalib with Goethe. The late Dr. Abdur Rahman Bijnauri considers his work as the second divine revelation. The works of Ghalib have become a part of the daily life of the Urdu speaking people of India and Pakistan. But it is regret table that the poetry of Ghalib is devoid of any social message which could better the lot of humanity. It was the characteristics of the time in which Ghalib flourished. But there is no doubt that Ghalib was a great artistic genius.

14. Ghalib was not only an Urdu poet, he was also a Persian poet. Ghalib was a great poet in Persian. His Persian quatrains are a fine blend of the sad and the sweet of life. But he is predominently an Urdu poet, not a Persian poet.

XXXIII

IMAM MALIK

1.   Medina was the centre of learning and culture in those days, and in Medina flourished some of the greatest scholars and intellectual giants of those times.

The celebrated Imam Malik was one of them. He was a great traditionist and scholar.

2.   Imam Malik was the founder of the Maliki School of Fikh and has left ineffaceable legacy in the field of Muslim learning. His well-known book "Muatta" occupies an outstanding place among the books of traditions. Being a teacher of exceptional merit, he holds a unique position in the Islmaic history as the founder and architect of the Maliki School, which has wielded a great influence on the contemporary and the later generations of Muslims, particularly on the Muslims of Africa and Spain.

3.   He was gifted with an indomitable will and incorruptable character and he never yielded, even to the whims or caprices of the highest authorities of the state. The Imam Malik ranked among a class of early Muslims whose lives would always serve as shining lights to those who strive for the realisation of nobler and higher virtues and saintly characters in life in this world.

4.   Malik Ibn Anas belonged to a respectable Arab family holding high social position in Medina. His ancestor came from Yemen, but his anchestors converted to Islam settled in Medina. His grandfather Abu Amir was the first in his family to adopt Islam in 2 A.H. According to the historian Ibn Khallikan, Malik was born in 95 A.H. but according to others he was born in 93 A.H., being younger by 13 years to famous Imam Abu Hanifa.

He received education in Medina which was then the greatest centre of learning and culture in the vast Muslim empire, and where lived most of the distinguished companions of the Prophet. He never went out of Medina to acquire knowledge. His father, grandfather and uncles all were traditionists. They taught the young Malik in traditions and other branches of learning. The other illustrious intellectual luminaries from whom the young Imam acquired knowledge were famous Imam Jaffar Sadiq, Muhammad Bin Shahal Az Zuhri, Nafe Yahya Bin Sahid and Rabia.

5.   When Imam Malik was an infant, his father Anas was called by the Caliph to join the army and he remained there as a soldier for 22 years. Imam Malik was brought up and educated by his mother who was a great intelligent lady. When his father was relieved of army duties on his return to Medina he found his son a great learned scholar who used to give lectures to a vast concourse every day.

6.   Imam Malik was a great teacher and a savant throughout his life. He was a teacher devoted to the noble cause of education for 62 years. He died on 11th Rabiul-Auwal at the matured age of 86 years.

7.   The great name and fame of Imam Malik as a teacher and a profound scholar spread far and wide and students, scholars and seekers of knowledge came to him for acquisition of knowledge from all over the Muslim world. He produced many learned scholars from among his pupils and many were benefited from his learning. Among the persons who profited by his learning were Caliphs Mansur, Mehdi, Hadi, Harun, Mamun, legists like Imam Abu Hanifa, Imam Shafai, Sufian Sauri, Qazi Yusuf, and scholars like Ibn Shahab Zuhri, and Yahya Bin Sa'eed Bin Fazil Bin Abbas. According to reliable records the number of his pupils who acquired fame for learning and scholarship in life was thirteen hurndred more or less.

8.   Imam Malik was a great disciplinarian as a teacher. His classes were characterised for their calm serenity, discipline, and by a high sense of respect shown by pupils to their teacher. He never tolerated any act of indiscipline. Once the Abbasid Caliph

Mansoor who was discussing certain traditions spoke a little loudly. The Imam rebuked him saying— "Do not raise your voice when you discuss". He refused to teach tradition in the camps of Caliphs.

9. Imam's Work:

The Imam left behind him more than a dozen books. Among them "Muatta" is the most famous. In the opinion of Shah Waliullah this book is a collection of the most authentic traditions of the holy Prophet sorted out after sifting enquiries as to their sources. In its revised edition it contains 1720 traditions and Muatta has been translated into various languages.

10. Imam Malik as a traditionist holds a unique place among the galaxy of such vast scholars and traditionists like Bukhari and Imam Muslim. It is said that the great Imam never sat except in the company of the highly learned personalities. In the opinion of Imam Hanbal Imam Malik has acquired unique distinction in the field of tradition. He never accepted any tradition unless he was fully satisfied of its genuineness.

Imam Malik had to undergo great hardships for acquisition of knowledge. It is recorded that Imam Bukhari had to live on roots and herbs of forest now and then. Imam Malik had to sell the beams of his house in order to bear the expenses of his education. He often said:— "One does not attain the heights of intellectual glory unless he is faced with chill penury. Poverty school in which the man's hidden energies, potentialities and the hard virtues are developed and enables him to surmount all odds and obstacles.

11. His contemporaries and the later traditionist and religious scholars all held very high opinion about the high intellectual attainments of Imam Malik. Besides being a traditionist he was also a great legist and gave fatwas in Medina for more than sixty years.

12. Imam Malik's Character:

Imam Malik was known for his transparent, honesty, integrity and great piety. He always lived up to his own conviction and he never deviated from the right path by any consideration, favour or gain and was never brow beaten or cowed down by fear or threat of fear or frown fret or foam from any person however powerful and influencial. He was one of those rare true Muslims who could never be purchased and indomitable courage, unbending rectitude characterised his whole life.

13.   When the Imam was 52 years of age, the caliphate passed into the hands of the Abbasids, among whom, the Caliph Mansoor was his colleague and he respected him highly for his profound learning. But the Imam did not side with him. When the people informed him that they had taken the oath of fealthy for the caliphate of Mansoor, the Imam boldly declared that Mansoor had forced the people to take the oath of allegiance to him, so it is not binding. The Imam quoted the tradition of the Prophet that a divorce by force is not legal.

14.   The Imam was a man of great moral character. He did not fear any mortal except Allah. Ja'far, a cousin of Caliph Mansoor was appointed the Governor of the city of Medina. He forced the people to renew their oath of fealthy to the Caliph Mansoor and he asked the Imam Malik not to issue the fatwa that a forced divorce is not legal. But the Imam, a man of firm conviction did not obey the governor's order. The governor was enraged and ordered that 70 stripes should be inflicted on Imam. 70 stripes inflicted on the naked body of the Imam and blood flowed profusely, to further humiliate him Imam with his bloody body was paraded through the streets of Medina. When the Caliph Mansoor came to know of this cruelty on the pious Imam, he punished his governor and apologised to the Imam.

15.   The Imam was above all earthly temptation. Once the Caliph Mansoor sent three thousand dinars to Imam Malik as his travelling expense to Bagdad; but he refused the money and did not agree to stir out from Medina, the city of the holy Prophet.

16.   The Imam feared Allah only and no earthly power. In 174 A.H. the celebrated Abbaside Caliph Harun-ar-Rashid arrived in Medina with his two sons, Amin and Mamun. Harun called the Imam Malik to his Darbar to deliver lectures on Muatta. The Imam

flatly declined to discuss Muatta in his Darbar and told the Caliph: "Rashid ! tradition forms a branch of learning which was cultivated by your ancestors and unless you pay due respect to it, who would do pay such respect?" The Caliph was convinced and preferred to attend the classes of the Imam held at his residence like any other commoner.

17.   The Imam was known for self-control and had a boundless resource of patience and edurance. Once a band of Kharijites armed with swords forced their way into the Mosque of Kufa where Imam Malik was praying. All worshippers left the mosque in panic but the Imam did not move from his seat. These fanatical Kharijites were so pleased with the answer of the Imam to their question, that they left the mosque satisfied leaving the Imam undisturbed. The Caliph Mansoor made it a rule that whoever visited him, he should kiss the hands of the Caliph. The Imam declared this custom as humiliating and derogatory but the Imam never refrained from showing proper respect to the learned people. He offered his own seat when Imam Abu Hanifa came to meet him. Duirng his Medina visit the celebrated Harun-ar-Rashid wished to attend the lectures of Muatta by Imam Malik. He sent for the Imam but the Imam replied:— "People come in search of knowledge but knowledge does not seek people". Harun-ar-Rashid came himself to attend the class and wanted others to leave the class but the Imam refused down right saying : "I can not sacrifice the interest of common men for that of an individual." So the Caliph with his two sons had to take their seats with the common people and listened with them to the very learned discourses of the Imam.

18.   The greatness and the nobility of the Imam Malik does not lie only in his being a founder of the Malik School of law, but in his being the greatest intellectual giant of the early Islam. The Imam was known for his piety, integrity and profound scholarship and high learning, above all he was a model man of character with great moral strength.

XXXIV

JABIR IBN HAYYAN

1.   The early history of Islam is full of brilliant records of the glorious achievements of Muslim poets, philosophers, historians, chemists, astronomers, doctors, physicians, mathematicians, geometricians etc.

Chemistry is one of the sciences, to which the Muslims have made the greatest contribution. The Muslims developed the science of chemistry to such a high degree of perfection that the Muslims may be called the founder of the science of chemistry.

2.   Mr. Phillip K. Hitti acknowledge the greatness of the Arabs in chemistry. In his book— "A history of the Arabs Hitti" writes—After materia medica astronomy and mathematics the Arabs made their greatest scientific contribution in chemistry and other physical sciences. The Arabs introduced the objective experiment, a decided improvement over the hazy speculation of the Greek. Accurate in the observation of phenomena and diligent in the accumulation of facts, the Arabs nevertheless found it difficult to project proper hypothesis.

3.   Another renowned European author in his famous book— "Making of Humanity" writes—while frankly admitting of debts of the science of chemistry to the Muslims— "chemistry, the rudiments of which arose in the process employed by the European metallurgist and jewellers combining metals inot various alloys and tinting them to resemble gold—process long preserved as a long secret monopoly of the priestly college and clad in the usual mystic formulae, developed in the hands of the Arabs into a widespread, organised passion for research which led them to the invention of distillation, sublimation, infiltration, to the discovery

of alcohol of nitric and sulphuric acid, of the alkalis, of the salts of mercury, of antimony and bismuth and laid the basis of all subsequent chemistry and physical research".

4.   Jabir's early life

Abu Musa Jabir Ibn Hayyan Al Azdi called Sufi and well-known as "Geber" in the West, was born in Tus in 721 A.C. According to other version Jabir flourished in Kufa in about 776 A.C. and was celebrated as the father of chemistry. Along with Zakriya Razi, he stands as the greatest name in the Annals of chemical science. His father Hayyan was a druggist by profession and belonged to the south Arabian famous tribe of Al-Azd. Hayyan who had settled in Kufa was an enthusiastic supporter of the Abbasside Caliphate. At the time of Jabir's birth his father was in Persia as an Abbasside agent. Soon after Hayyan was arrested and executed by the Ommayyid officers. So young Jabir was sent to Arabia where he received his early education. Jabir received his education from the Ommayyid Prince Khalid Ibn Yazid Ibn Muawiyah and from the celebrated Imam Ja'far Al-Sadiq.

5.   As a youth, Jabir was a devoted pupil of Ja'far Sadeq who was then a very famous professor of Alchemy and Astrology. Later on, it is said, he joined the Sufi order founded by Abu Hashim of Kufa. In the beginning of his life Jabir practised as a physician and was intimately associated with the house of Barmekide, which supplied the powerful ministers of the Caliph Harun-ar-Rashid and the members of which held high posts during the reign of Harun-ar-Rashid.

6.   Jabir too had to share the misfortune of the Barmekides at the time of their downfall in 803 A.C. and went back to Kufa from Bagdad and spent the rest of his life there. According to some authority he died in 813 A.C. during the reign of Mamun and according to others he died in 800 A.C.

7.   Jabir's famous chemical laboratory at Kufa was discovered after two centuries of his death during the excavation for building in a quarter near the Damascus Gate. A large piece of gold was also found near his laboratory.

8. Jabir's Works

Jabir was versatile genius and a prolific writer. He is credited with the composition of more than 100 books, of which 22 books on chemical science are still extant. He introduced experimental research in chemical science which added greatly to its rapid development. Numerous treatise on medicine, astronomy, magic, philosophy etc. appear under his name.

9.   Jabir made a list of the titles of his books, which was reproduced in part by Ibn Al-Nadim in his Kitabul Fihrist, a Muslim encyclopaedia of the 10th century. About a hundred of Jabir's books are reported to exist either in manuscripts on or native lithographs in various libraries of Europe and Asia. Two surving works of Jabir are still extant, of which (1) Kitab-Al Rahman (the book of mercy), (2) Kitab-Al Mulk (the book of kingdom), (3) Kitab-Al Mawazin-Al Saghir (little book of balance), (4) Kitab-Al Tajmi (the book of concentration), (5) Kitab-Al Zibag Al-Shagri (the book of easter mercury) are most well-known. The fame of Jabir rests on his alchemical books in Arabic. His book of Kingdom and little book of Balance have been published.

10.   George Sarton writes about his books: "We find in them remarkably sound views on the method of chemical research, a theory on the geological formations of metals; the so-called sulpher-mercury theory of metals (the six metals) differ essentially because of different proportions of sulpher and arsenic and antimony in their sulphides. Jabir deals also with various applications of th refinement of metals, preparation of steel, dyeing of cloth and leather, varnishes to waterproof cloth and protect iron the use of manganese dioside in glass making, the use of iron pyrites for writing in gold, the distillation of vinegar to concentrate acetic acid. He observed the imponderability of magnetic force."

11.   Jabir laid great stress on the importance of experimentation in his researches, hence he made a great advancement in chemical science. Western writers credit Jabir with the discovery of many new chemical compounds.

12. Max Meyerhof says

"His (Jabir's) influence may be traced throughout the whole historic course of European alchemy and chemistry."

Mr. K. Hitti in his book "A history of the Arabs" writes— "The works to which his (Jabir's) name was attached, were, after the 14th century the most influential chemical treatise both in Europe and Asia...... Jabir modified and corrected the Aristotelian theory of the constituents of metal which remaind unchanged till the beginning of modern chemistry in the 18th century A.C. He was explained in his works the preparations of many chemical substances such as cinnabar (sulphide of mercury) and arseṅious oside. It has been proved that Jabir was conversant with the preparations of nearly pure vitriols, alums, and alkalis and the production of the so-called liver and milk of sulpher. He prepared mercury oxide and crude sulphuric and nitric acids and he knew the method of the solution of gold and silver with acid.

13. Jabir is also the author of a book on the astrolabe and has written several treatises on spherical trigonometry.

14. Jabir's treatises have been translated in various European languages and have exercised a deep and lasting influence on the entire course of the development of the modern science of chemistry.

His coined chemical words still in vogue are: "Realgar (red sulphide of arsenic), tutia (zinc oxide), alkali, antimony (Arabic ithemid), alembic, sal-amonica.

15. Richard Russel (1678) an English translator ascribes a book called "Sun of Perfection" to Jabir and calls Jabir as "the most famous Arabian Prince and philosopher". Albert of Bollstaidt (Albertus Magnus) and Roger Bacon have incorporated many of Jabir's theories in their works. "The influence of Jabir is very much pronounced" — says an European writer in the "Encyclopaedia speculum maturale" by Vincent de Beauvais.

16. In 1893 nine small works of Jabir were edited and translated by O' Hondas and published by Berthelot. The most important

books of Mr. Jabir beside those already mentioned above are the great book of properties, the three books of the elements of foundation and a book of poison.

17. The description of mineral acids by Jabir, which was transmitted to the Western world is considered to be the most important piece of information contained in his work. He has also described numerous methods of testing metals. Jabir had a clear grasp of his theories and this is why his works were used as text books for chemists many centuries after the death of Jabir till the 18th century.

Jabir's influence on the science of chemistry is still admitted by almost all authorities on the science of chemistry.

XXXV

PRINCESS ZAIBUN NISSA

1. The Mughul ladies were highly educated and accomplished. Babur's wife, sisters and aunts all were educated and accomplished. Though there were very few female schools and colleges the Muslim kings, emperors and other great men and nobles made perfect arrangements for proper education of their daughters and other female relatives.

Though historians have given no special place in their histories for the Princes and Princes of a Muslim king or emperor but some of them by their charms, fascination, intellectual and literary accomplishments have attracted the special attention of historians, authors and writers and biographers could not ignore them as they acquired name and fame for their extraordinary achievements in life and in the literary world.

2. Princess Zaibun Nissa, the daughter of Emperor Aurangzeb was exceptionally brilliant literary genius and also as a poetess.

She was born in 1048 A.H., in the second year of the marriage of Aurangzeb and Dilras Banu, daughter of Shah Nawaz Safvi, a Persian national who rose to high positions during the reign of Shah Jehan.

3. Zaibun Nissa was a born genius. Even in her early girlhood she was able to recite the Quran in an exquisitely mastery manner to the surprise of all. Her accomplishment so charmed her father Emperor Aurangzeb that he announced a reward of 3,000 gold coins for her. It is an admitted fact that Zaibun Nissa was highly learned and erudite in Persian and Arabic literature and possessed a superb caligraphy. Her great learning attracted to Aurangzeb's court such learned men as Mullah Saeed and Mullah Ashraf, two

famous scholars of that age. They were engaged to teach Zaibun Nissa and she received instruction both in prose and poetry.

4. Due to her artistic tendency and her attraction for literary works she had no liking for politics. She did not marry and died in 1113 A.H. Aurangzeb had great affection for her. He burst into tears when he heard the news of the death of Zaibun Nissa.

5. She had a great influence upon her father. Her joyful nature amiable character and jubilant spirit greatly helped her father in her dealings with others. She was quite indifferent to worldly charms and had a fair and impartial views of every matter. Kashmir with its natural sceneries and beauties had a great charm for her.

6. She had extreme affection for brothers, cousins and other relations. Her tombstone bears the inscription "Udkhuli Jannati". She possessed spotless character. She lived her life according to a fixed programme which received royal assent every week. This programme included hours of meals, studies, baths, prayers, tutorials, other functions such as visits to gardens, holy places, visits to relatives etc. She never wore perfumed, scented or luxurious clothes when she went to meet her father Aurangzeb.

7. Zaibun Nissa performed five daily prayers and Tahajjud (mid-night) prayer also. Her teachers were elderly people, well-versed in the Quran and Hadith and they were also well-versed in sociology and psychology. She received a very sound education in theology and art of knowledge. Her father Aurangzeb was a model Muslim and he took all the care to bring Zaibun Nissa up a ideal Muslim girl.

8. Aurangzeb imprisoned Zaibun Nissa because she supported Prince Moazzam against the will of her father and for no other fault of her own. Her pure and spotless character has been maliciously impugned by concocted tales, and cooked up stories. These figments of perverted imagination are mere concoctions and got up false stories have been repeated by some writers and these imaginary and fanciful tales and false romantic stories have come down to us.

9.   No doubt Zaibun Nissa was a poet of the first order, but all the diwans and verse depicting her supposed romance with Aqil Khan ascribed to her are sheer forgeries and later concoctions and never composed by her. These verses cannot be true. She was a pious lady and true Muslim. The Persian historian who came to Delhi during her time, has not mentioned any romance about her, and she lived under the eye of her father, the stern Emperor Aurangzeb.

10.   Accounts rendered by foreign ambassadors about Aurangzeb's court and the palace do not mention these romances about Zaibun Nissa. Had there been any iota of truth what-so-ever, they would have mentioned these in their descriptions of Mughul court. All contemporary historians have not recorded any such romantic stories about Zaibun Nissa. There is nothing about these romantic tales in the imperial record office at New Delhi. The India office library also does not furnish any bases for these false fabrications. Even in the works of J.N. Sarkar there is nothing to testify to the truth of these vile calumnies about the spotless character of Zaibun Nissa. Even the most hostile historian Kafi Khan who in his history has tried to blacken the reign of Aurangzeb by his designed false records and versions (as being a Shia, he was a bitter enemy of Sunni Aurangzeb) has not mentioned them in his history. Darbar-e-Akbaree also do not mention these fabricated stories.

11.   Upto date no reliable and authentic records have been found or discovered to corroborate these forged cooked up, concocted false imaginary vile calumnies about this great Princess of extraordinary intellectual attainments. These concoctions must be the works of those vile creatures who were out to blacken the good name and fame of the Emperor Aurangzeb out of enmity, jealousness and malice towards him.

XXXVI

BAHADUR SHAH ZAFAR

(The last of the Mughul Emperor)

1. The history of Abu'l Muzaffar Serajuddin Muhammad Bahadur Shah Zafar is the history of the last fading glory of the Mughul dominion in India of the fleeting kingship and elusive power, punctuated by painful consciousness of abject submission and enforced surrender to the dictates of a cruel irony of fate which ran its inexorable course during a short span of less than three decades.

2. Bahadur Shah Zafar as he is popularly known was the last emperor of the Mughul dynasty in India. He was a lineal descendants of Taimur Lang the world conqueror and second son of Akbar Shah II. Bahadur Shah was born in October 1775 and succeeded to the throne of Delhi in the sun set of his life in September 1837 when he was an old man of 70 years of age.

3. Though an emperor in name and symbol and pivot of unity and royal dignity, he was reduced to a mere figure head by varied forces of circumstances, worked out by a cruel destiny. He was a Sultan of Delhi receiving a pension of rupees one lakh per month from the East India Company.

4. There is no doubt that Bahadur Shah was the best fitted of Akbar II's sons to succeed his father. He was the best of the Mughul kings after Aurangzeb.

The shadow has brightened and darkened his fame and turned the philosopher poet Bahadur Shah in the eye of some biased and prejudiced writers into the alleged scheming rebel against British rule. He was of 82 years of age when the Mutiny broke out in 1857.

When the soldiers of the national freedom movement approached him, he wanted to retire to the shrine of Kutub Saheb as a religious devotee. He has been villified by most non-Muslim and English writers. He maintained his dignity and traditional etiquette.

5.   Bahadur Shah appears throughout as a man of cultured and upright character. In 1806 when he was thirty-two years old and his father was trying to pass him over in favour of Jehangir, he was described as a very respectable character by Seton. Twenty years later Charles Met Calfe none too a friendly critic where the Mughuls are concerned thus wrote of him— "I have always advised heir apparent (Bahadur Shah) to submit with patience to the will of his royal father. I must add that his conduct is in every respect highly creditable to him. He is undoubtedly the most respectable, the most accomplished of the princes, the most worthy of his majesty's love and although it is withheld from him I have never known him to deviate from the observance of proper respect and fitial duty (vide twilight of the Mughuls by Percival Spear, fellow of Salwen college Cambridge: page 73 (1951 edition).

6.   Bahadur Shah as a prince lived and dressed simply. He was described at the same time a man of spare figure and stature. From palace diary and official records it appears that Bahadur Shah sometimes spent whole days in reading, writing and studying the Quran and composing verses in the Roshanara garden. Bahadur Shah was educated to the life of a mediatized prince and the role fitted him very well. But as a philosopher he would have adorned any court. Delhi in his time was an Indian Weimer Ghalib for its Goethe. His (Bahadur Shah's) interest and tastes were primarily literary and aesthetic. He loved poetry and philosophy, gardens and nature in all its guises. He enjoyed gardens and himself laid out two. He loved animals. He had special fondness for doves. He was religious without being fanatical and learned without being pedantic. He was no bigot, but above all Bahadur Shah was a poet and a literary patron. He was a pupil and friend of poet Zauk. He was a great literary genius. Bahadur Shah did not suffer from the usual vice of his race—addiction to strong drink but he shared their taste for good things of life. Taking all in all Bahadur Shah presents a

pleasing figure, if not a heroic figure. He possessed real abilities and had the courage of his race. (vide Ibid page 73,74 and 75).

7.   At page 75 Mr. Percival Spear in his book Twilight of the Mughuls remarks— "His (Bahadur Shah's) later misfortunes brought a quality of stoic endurance of suffering which must inspire respect in the least friendly judged by the evidence available, by the standard of his time and in relation to the peculiar difficulties of his position. Bahadur Shah stands as a dignified, cultured, intellectual and not unsympathetic figure. He lies in Rangoon, far from the city that he loved, but his memory, alone of the Mughuls since Aurangzeb is still verdant among the people. He continues— "The later Mughuls maintained the etiquette of the court in all its rigour so far as they were able. The miniatures and ivory paintings of the time depict the solemn procession through the streets in which the court delighted on great occasions such as religious festivals or a royal wedding. The king or his representative always attended the Jamah Mosque on the Ids or religious festivals. The king mounted on an elephant with the royal princes and the chief noble men in behind, with foot and horse in front and rear, the party made a brave show with its gaily coloured trappings, its bejewelled figures and the scarlet uniforms of the soldiers, trumpets and kettle drums went before and the scene was enjoyed as much by the citizens as the courtiers themselves. Within the palace there were the durbars. The public durbars were held in the Dewani Khas, the larger in the Diwan-i-Aam".

8.   At page 83 Percival writes— "The court under Bahadur Shah was a cultural influence of great value. With the royal patronage it became the centre of the second period of Urdu literature whose highest star was the great Ghalib. By its patronage it kept alive the Delhi School of painting which produced at least two painters of merit in Raja Jivan Ram and Hussain Nazir. The end of the court involved a break in cultural as well as political tradition and ushered the Garish period of utility into Indian life. The court of Delhi, faded though it was, had more in it than the Tinsel fo Khelats and the honorofics of Shugats. It was the refuge of a traditional culture whose tragedy it was largely to perish at the hand of the political passion and misplaced alien benevolence."

9.   When the historic war of independence broke out in 1857, Bahadur Shah had hardly completed two decades of his uneventful rule. The glorious role played by Bhadur Shah in this great fight for the national liberation from an imperialistic domination has ensured him a befitting place in the galaxy of the heroes for national liberation of the then India. So Subas Chandra Bose has rightly said— "Bahadur was the last fighter for India's freedom; the man was an emperor among men and a man among emperors."

10.   Bahadur showed realism of compassion, fellow-feeling and liberality in the battle of Delhi. At one stage when the indian soldiers captured 60 British women and children and brought them before Bahadur Shah, he said— "Our religion rigorously forbids the slaying of women and children. Lodge them comfortably in the fort, give them food and clothing, and look after them in a fitting manner."

11.   It was on September 14, 1857 the four-month old warfare between the Indian liberation forces and the Britis came to an end. As the English forces accompanied by the Gurkha troops were scaling the walls of Delhi Fort, Bahadur Shah rode on horse back and reached the spot known as Lal Duggi where the entire army and the populace had assembled for his address.

On Septemeber 19, 1857 Bahadur Shah and the whole royal family evacuated the fort and took asylum in the tomb of their ancestor Emperor Humayun.

12.   The reign of terror upon which the British army embarked following the capture of Delhi is still a heart rending tales of woes and cruelties unparalled in the dark catalogue of human crimes. On imaginary charges of treason and espionage, the pick of the nobility was exiled; properties of hundreds of them consficated: their wives and children dishonoured. The house of suspect. Hindu or Muslim was razed to the ground. Countless innocent women, rich or poor with hair dishavelled ran out screaming towards the outlying towns and villages. No food was available in the city in which a few months ago articles of food were abundant and cheap— the rate of wheat was about forty seers per rupee and the rate of ghee was four seers per rupee and so on. Tens of thousands

died of hunger and disease. According to the famous historian Jadu Nath Sarkar— "Within the four walls of old Delhi nearly a lakh of houses were completely destroyed by the conquering British army giving it an appearance of a Atom-bomb city."

13. When the orgy of bloodshed and vandalism was over, two English officers—one of whom was Hodson brought out the aged Emperor Bahadur Shah and his sons and other family members from the Humayun's tomb. The old emperor was confined in the house of Nazir Hussain Mirza while the princes were cruelly shot dead by the order of Hodson. Soon after Bahadur Shah was tried for abetment of murder and declared guilty by a bogus trial and in December 1857 was exiled to Rangoon where he died on November 7, 1862, bequeathing to the British like Nepolion, the shame of his death.

14. Bahadur Shah was a scholar, a poet and a calligrapher and his Diwan is a priceless volume in Urdu. Some of his odes bristle with anticipation of misfortunes which made their appearance with soulless cruelties. The period of his incarceration in Rangoon brought out all the pathos and patriotism of his poetic mind. With a prophetic version he wrote— "The misfortunes of Zafar knew no bounds, even after death he could not procure two yards of land in the country of his origin". It is a fact that permission to bury him in India was refused by the British. He further prophesed in his pathetic verses— "Can any one offer fateha at Zafar's grave? Most certainly not. For whatever traces were left of a dilapidated tomb have been stamped out by the strokes of human kicks". It is a fact that for a long time Bahadur Shah's grave could not be traced out and even the present supposed site of his grave is uncertain. His prophecy has come out to be true. He said in his odes— "Fate doomed is flickering candle lighted on my grave. The icy hand of the howling wind will put it out, even before the approaching night."

15. An English writer Percival Spear in his book "Twilight of the Muguls" at page 218 has given a graphic description of the conditions of citizens of Delhi after the capture of Delhi by the British army in these glowing words— "For the citizens of Delhi the after-math of the Mutiny was a case of the scorpions of

Rehoboam following the whips of Solomon. Under military rule they had been subjected to shortages and insecurity, to extortion and plunder but for the few weeks after the capture they were evicted from the city altogether and liable to summary execution at sight. Hindus and Muslims were at first indiscriminately killed. In the city no man's life was safe. All able bodied men who were seen were taken for rebels and shot." "The troops" wrote Saunder himself "Were completely disorganised and demoralised by the immense amount of plunder which fell into their hands". After this first collapse, the reaction of exhausted and over-wrought men, there followed a more systematic reign of terror which lasted for several weeks. "The whole population was at first driven out"— Mrs. Saunders wrote in the same letter of 25 Octorber. "Every house in the city was desolute and many of them injured. The inhabitants of this huge place seven miles round are dying daily of starvation and want of shelter". There was much indiscriminate shooting beside drum head court martials and summary hangings. There were many cases like that of Hazi who was cut down by an officer at Nizamuddin Aulia's Tomb without a word of enquiry. The Delhi Gazetter of 1883-4 records the case of a village which had given up a servant of Sir John Met Calfe to the king. In retaliation twenty-one of the leading villagers were summarily shot. A gallow was set up and fed with five or six victims a day. An idea of the magnitude of the operation can be gathered from the fact that the special commission set up to deal with offenders tried summarily 3,306 persons of whom 2,025 were convicted of those 392 were hanged. The shooting of the three princes by Hudson in cold blood was the typical instance."

16. Mr. Percival at pages 222-24 continues— "Bahadur Shah was tried by a military court. The trial lasted from January 27 to March 9,1858. The supreme government decreed his removal to Rangoon. The formal charges were four in number that; he aided and abetted Muhammad Bakht Khan in rebellion, that he aided and abetted his son Mirza Mughul in a similar rebellion, that being a subject of the British Government, he proclaimed himself sovereign of India and waged war against Government and that he was responsible for the death of fortynine Europeans, mostly women and children on 16th May. The defence was too cowed to put

forward the juristic argument of still subsisting imperial Mughul rights and it was left to a British scholar more than sixty years later to maintain that it was really the company which had rebelled against the king (Bahadur Shah)."

All these charges against Bahadur Shah were not proved.

17. Bahadur Shah Zafar was a fascinating personality and his was a life of proud eminence and tragic dignity. Though not conceiveably, with any appreciation of the modern democracy he had for diverse reasons come to symbolise in his person and the approaching doom of his high office, the fears, hopes pangs and aspirations of a people that now seem to have lived too long under the shadow of illusions.

The personal tragedy of the last Mughul Emperor who was in humanely treated by his victors and who before his sad end as a destitute in far away Rangoon had the brutal horror an agony of witnessing the most sadistic slaughter of his own sons and daughters.

The uprising of 1857, was the culmination of complex social forces and though it failed to achieve its purpose immediately and even released a wave of ruthless oppression from which Muslims of the then India took long to recover, its character and consequence was wider than can be encompassed by the life and death of a great king, glorious though his name and heroic his inspiring example.

XXXVII

SOME GREAT QUEENS

1. The simultaneous rule in the thirteenth century of the three famous Muslim Queens—namely Sultana Razia Begum of India, Shahajar-Ad-Dur of Egypt, and Begum Abish of Iran appears to be very interesting mystery; one is not able to understand the nature of this strange coincidence.

Sultana Razia

The detailed life of Sultana Razia has been narrated supra. Sultan Altamish was well aware of the unfitness of his sons to succeed him. So he nominated his daughter Razia as his successor. Sultana Razia ascended the throne of Delhi after her father's death and reigned 3½ years with great ability and lustre in spite of the fact that the condition of Northern India was not peaceful at that time. Though a woman, Sultana Razia possessed the vigour and indomitable energy. Wearing the robes of a Sultan, she sat on the throne, gave daily audience and administered justice without concealing her face. She rode on an elephant through the cheering crowds and attended the mosque regularly on every Friday. She led her troops to many battles and her historical accounts are full of how she herself fought against the enemies. Her manliness and heroism together with the courage and the burning spirit were incomparable. Razia was the only Muslim Queen who ruled over India with such a consummate skill and valour. She was a great learned princess and most beautiful lady. It was her misfortune that she was a female queen. She reigned 3½ years. Her rule was popular and renowned for the removal of many abuses. The historian Hasan Nizami in his history has given a good account of her and has extolled her in these words— "Sultana Razia was a great monarch, wise, just, generous, a benefactor of her realms, a dispenser of equity, the protector of her people, and the leader of her armies; she had all the kingly qualities except sex, and this exception made all her virtues of no effect in the eye of men. May God have mercy upon her."

Queen Shahajar-Ad-Dur of Egypt

1. In the year 639 the Muslims conquered Egypt, and several Muslim dynasties ruled over Egypt. After the destruction of the Ayyubite dynasty in 1250 A.C. the Bahri and Burjee Mamelukes reigned in Egypt.

2. Shahajar-Ad-Dur was the first ruler of the Bahre mameluke dynasty. She was the Queen of Nazimuddin Saleh, Salah-Ud Aldin's grand nephew.

3. Four important crusades were fought during the 13th century. The Crusader Luis IX. King of France led the crusading expedition when the Egyptian Queen Shahajar-Ad-Dur was at the height of her power. From their previous experience they realised that unless the Muslim rule in Egypt was destroyed, the Christian rule over Zerusalem would not be safe. So Luis IX with vast Crusading forces invaded Egypt by sea and gained preliminary success in Egypt.

4. At the critical moment when the Crusading forces under Luis were advancing on Cairo, Nizamuddin, husband of Shahjar-Ad-Dur died, but the brave Queen Shahjar-Ad-Dur kept the news of the Sultan's death a guarded secret and herself with remarkable zeal and vigour led the Muslim army in person against the Christian forces.

5. Both the armies met in grim battle at Fariskur on 6th April 1250 A.C. The Queen, by her wonderful valour and tact and by her inspiring personality and strategy inflicted a crushing defeat on the Christian Crusaders and imprisoned their supreme commander Luis IX.

6. She was a noble and chivalrous Muslim Queen. Though sorely tried and bitterly harrassed by Luis and his Crusading

forces, she rose equal to Islam's great injunction and displayed chivalry and tolerance of Luis when he sought peace and spared the life of Luis very generously. This is a great example of noble forgiveness to a mortal enmey which is rarely met in human history.

Then an era of glory and despair followed during her reign but her last days were quiet and she passed away in peace. She was a great Queen who rose by dint of her merit from the position of a slave girl to the highest position of a queen. She was the brave Queen who saved Egypt for Islam. Had the Crusaders succeeded to destroy Muslim power in Egypt; Syria and Hedjaj would have fallen an easy prey to Christendom; and Islam would have been suppressed even in Asia and Africa. So the historical value of Queen Shahajar-Ad-Dur's great victory is great and immense and far reaching.

Queen Abish

1. The Queen Abish was a great Queen of Persia. She ruled in Persia at a time when the condition of Persia was very chaotic.

2. The Queen Abish belonged to the Sala Gharid dynasty. She ascended the throne of Fars Salaghar, a Turkish General was the founder of this dynasty.

3. The Queen Abish married Mangu Taimur, the son of Halaku, sovereign of Persia who ruled over Persia from 1256 to 1265. Under the able rule of Halaku, her father-in-law, Abish had nothing to fear. The Queen Abish ruled over Fars for 25 years with great vigour and ability and with splendour even after the death of her father-in-law Halaku. In 1287 the brave Queen passed away among the lamentation of her people.

4. In those days Muslim women took parts in all walks of life. The well-known English Orientalist Sir E. Denison Ross in his history of Gujrat writes— "Sultan Mahmud trained women for various walks of life and employed them in all his offices. They constituted his bodyguard

and dressed and equipped like soldiers and these women soldiers accompanied him in his hunting expedition."

5. The literary Muslim women of the middle ages had not been content with their own personal passive intellectual and educational movements but took part in the intellectual and educational movements of the time. They delivered the regular course of lectures in important educational institutions, on important books, traditions, law, and literature and thousands of people attended their lectures.

   Ibn Batuta, the famous Muslim traveller in his travel book has mentioned the name of such lecturer women at Damascus and he says that he attended such lectures at Damascus. There are manuscripts in which the names of such women lecturers and literary women are recorded. There are three such manuscripts in the Khuda Buksh Oriental Public Library of Patna. In one of them, the names of more than fifty women are mentioned.

6. The woman was looked as a respectable being equal to man since Islam's beginning to the 17th century. History records that the Muslim women actually commanded armies in the fields and displayed bravery and skillfulness in archery and swordsmanship to such extent that it astounded the then world.

7. Muslim women in that age held the posts of judge, qazis and decided legal cases; they controlled the exchequer; they acted as plenipotentiaries to negotiate peace between warring states; they were held as authorities on law (Muftis) on which their opinions were sought; they pursued various branches of arts and literature; and they travelled far and wide. They attended the lectures of learned men. They gained great fame as caligraphists and poets and excelled therein. Even when the authority of the Khalif was shaken the authority of the literary and learned Muslim women remained.

8. Many celebrated men like At Khattib of Bagdad, the famous biographer Abul Mahasin of Egypt, the celebrated

historian Al-Humaydi, the famous traditionist of Spain, all received their education from women.

In the 12th century Ibn Asukir's great biographical dictionary of eighty volumes contain the numerous names of women teachers.

In the 14th century one author has mentioned the name of more than 170 literary women. In the following two centuries many learned women flourished. The high standard of the attainments and culture of the Muslim women of that ages are mentioned in the literary, historical and biographical works of the time which have come down to us.

THE FIRST SIX MUGHUL EMPERORS OF INDIA

1. The reign of first six Mughal emperors—from Babur to Aurangzeb, forms a glorious chapter of Indian history—nay of the world history.

The first six kings of the Mughal dynasty in India were most brilliant and virile emperors. They ruled India with greatness for more than two centuries. These great rulers contributed greatly and gloriously to human progress and advancement. They introduced a system of just government—just for all—Muslims and non-Muslims—for the good of their people. They encouraged trade and commerce, and patronised and aided and helped the spread of knowledge and education among the people.

2. Science, culture and civilization progressed and advanced under the fostering care and patronage of the great Mughul rulers of Delhi which was the most magnificent city on earth. In those days the courts of the Mughul emperors presented a brilliant gathering of the best men of learning from all parts of the world. Their reigns were an unique era of light and enlightenment and splendour and brilliancy. Muslims valued manliness, valour, honour, dignity, Islamic prestige than their own selfish gain. All soldiers, scholars, non-scholars played their role in up-holding the great traditions of Islam and Islamic way of the life.

3. True to the glorious tradition of Islam the prince and the peasant, the high, the low, the rich and the poor all received cheap and equal justice. Courtesy, politeness, humility, charity, hospitality and liberality were the main virtues among others of the Muslims of those days. The Mughul emperors are no more but the splendid achievement of their time and their monuments in various places of India and Pakistan and glorious records of the glorious virtus of the Muslims of that age still out in the history of the world to adorn a page and to point out a lesson to us.

4.   Pakistan has inherited glorious tradition of Islam and the Mughul India. It is an ideological state brought into existence to apply the code of Islam in practical life. Its green flag with crescent moon and star revives vividly the memory of the golden era of Islamic rule with its brilliant culture, progress and advancement. It reminds all of the early days of Islam where justice was free and impartial and open to all, high and low. Muslim scholars, scientists, statesmen, administrators, writers, learned men are all in Pakistan are on the front rank to revive the glorious past of Islam in Pakistan.

5.   The great sons of Paikistan, as soliders, naval cadets and air men today present a great spectacle of discipline, courage, patriotism and devotion to Islam. They are the vanguard of this new Pakistan nation who are trying by their self-sacrifice to restore the glory of Muslim bravery, service and chivalry. Pakistan is marching rapidly on the parth of progress and a great and virile Pakistan nation is out to show the fundamental principles of Islam in practice which can only solve the knotty problem of the present world.

XXXVIII

BABUR (1482—1530 A.C.)

1. The first Mughul emperor in India was Zahiruddin Muhammad surnamed Babur or the Tiger. He was one of the descendants of Chengis Khan and of Taimur. Though inheriting only the small kingdom of Ferghona ultimately extended his dominion by conquest of Delhi and the greater part of Hindustan. He was born in 1482 A.C. and died in 1530 A.C. He passed the greater part of his life in desperate military expeditions. He was a great general and a profound stateseminent scholar in Arabic, Persian and Turki and Hindi. He was an elegent poet, a minute critic in all .... and in the elegance of diction and an exact observer of the statistical phenomena of every region he entered. He was a great admirer of beautiful prospects and fine flowers, and a devout Muslim— good humoured, brave, munificent and frank in his character. He would have excelled Henry IV if he were born in Europe.

2. Babur's father died in his childhood. Powerful enemies who were checked by Umar Shaikh Mirza now raised their head but Babur though young, with his father's fighting ability defeated his enemies. He was ambitious like Taimur and conceived larger power for him than his great ancestor Taimur.

3. Babur soon entered his career of conquest. He defeated Afghans in a fierce battle and occupied Kabul and introduced law and order in Afghanistan.

4. A few years later Babur made preparations to invade India, that rich and fertile land which attracted conquerors from Central Asia.

Babur started on his expedition to India with a well-trained well-armed army. After several attempts, he captured Ghazni and other cities and he and his army advanced as far as the river Indus, but he had to wait many years before he could capture the Punjab.

5.   Sultan Ibrahim Ludi was the Sultan of Delhi. He ruled with an iron hand and his subjects suffered much through his acts of injustice and cruelty but no person dared to raise voice against his oppressive taxation for fear of life. Even Ludi's ministers were disgusted with his unjust and inhumane rule. Doulat Khan Ludi, a chief in the Punjab, having been dissatisfied with the cruel rule of Ibrahim Ludi, secretly invited Babur to overthrow Ibrahim Ludi.

6.   Babur eagerly agreed to help Doulat Khan. He advanced with his army and captured Lahore and Dipalpur. Babur now made arrangements to attack Ibrahim Ludi but all on a sudden Doulat Khan withdrew his offer of military help, and Babur found that his army was too small to attack and defeat superior forces of Ibrahim Ludi. So he returned to Kabul.

7.   Babur was a man who was never daunted by any failure in life. After a year in 1526 he again marched with an army of 12,000 into India and the great battle of Panipath was fought fifty miles north of Delhi. Sultan Ibrahim, it is said, had an army of one lakh consisting of both infantry and cavalry, but Babur undismayed faced his opponent's vast army—ten times larger than his own. Babur was a master of strategy, and he saw his only hope in sudden attack on the enemy. As the leading ranks of Ibrahim's army advanced to attack the cavalry of Babur he ordered his cavalry to attack them in the rear.

8.   Babur's cavalry wheeled to one side to avoid the attack of Sultan's cavalry and attack the Sultan's horsemen from behind before they had time to rearrange their lines. Taken aback Sultan's commanders could not restore order and discipline. There was chaos and confusion. Thick clouds of dust and riderless horses added to the confusion. The Sultan's generals shouted their commands to their forces but their voices could not be heard owing to din and noise of battle.

9. Babur employed his cavalry with supreme tact and skill and allowed the enemy no time to recover from their bewilderment. Babur's troops rushed through Sultan's cavalry and attacked his infantry which was unable to check the charge of Babur's cavalry. Within a few hours Sultan's forces were defeated leaving thousands killed and injured. Babur won this historic battle by employing supreme tactics and strategy and he proved the truth of the Quranic saying—"Sometimes smaller number triumph over the large one with divine help".

10. Babur was a brave man and true Muslim. When heard from his officer Dilawar Khan that Sultan Ibrahim Ludi lay dead in the battle field, he visited his dead body and showed his respect to the dead and directed Dilawar Khan to give his dead body a decent and honourable burial at the spot he died.

11. Panipath in Indian history, has decided the fate of many nations. Here again the fate of a nation was decided. The Mughul Sultanate was established in India. Babur became the emperor of India but he was not exclusive ruler of India and he had to divide his time between India and Kabul. His Ministers and army were at first reluctant to stay in India as the climate of India did not suit them but Babur persuaded them to stay in India by giving large money.

12. Babur was not now free from all troubles. Many powerful chiefs still disputed his right to rule the Punjab. Rana Sanga, the chief of the Rajput clan and the ruler of Mewar was his most bitter enemy. Rana Sanga was a veteran soldier with fifty scores on his body. Babur foresaw that so long Rana Sanga contested his authority as emperor of India, he was not safe in his position. But Babur's Ministers advised him not to risk his reputation by going to war with such a powerful enemy as Rana Sanga. At this affront of his Ministers the brave soul of Babur cried out—**"No, if I quail and play coward in this case, what would the other Muslim kings of the world say about me? Will they not say I have surrendered my kingdom simply because I dreaded Rana Sanga, a Hindu Rajput? For a Muslim, such cowardice is unthinkable."**

13. The Armies of Babur and Rana Sanga met in the grim battle of Khanwah, about 20 miles from Agra. Though smaller in number, Babur's army defeated the large army of Rana Sanga by superior skill, bravery and tactics. The Rajputs were completely defeated.

14. As the Afghan chiefs of Bihar and Bengal did not submit to his sovereignty, he met them in a fierce battle near the Ghagra and won a decisive victory. Babur now was the undisputed emperor of India.

15. Bukhara and Samarkand were then the centres of Muslim culture and learning. Babur, the untiring warrior was a product of this cultural atmosphere. The Tozuk (Babur's autobiography) shows that his education could not have been meagre. He records that his leisure and rest were very scanty still he pursued his intellectual studies. He has left for us not only his wonderful autobiography but a dewan, a Masnavi and a journal in Turki verse. His Masnavi consists of two thousand couplets dealing with religious and moral topics and is said to have written for the education of his sons. He got his son Humayun and daughter Gulbadan well-educated under most adverse conditions. He invented a special script called Khate Baburi in which he wrote several copies of the Quran. He compiled a book on Hanifi Law.

16. The character of emperor Babur is most captivating. He combined in him a character of brave soldier and the intense love of knowledge and learning. He was happy both in combat and among books in his library. He could mix freely with his uneducated common soldiers as well as men of light and learning. He was physically strong and could lift a man in each hand and yet he could be as gentle and kind as a woman when he was by the side of a wounded comrade in a battle field. The hand of Babur which wielded a sword with deadly accuracy could also handle a pen for useful writing.

17. Babur has written an autobiography in excellent ways. In his memoir he writes about then India—"Hindustan is situated in the first, second and third climates and no part of it in the fourth. It is remarkably a fine country. It is quite a different world, as

compared with our countries. Its hills and rivers, its forests and plains, its inhabitants and their languages, its winds and rains are all of a different nature. Although the hot districts in the territory of Kabul bear in many respects some resemblance to Hindustan, while in other particulars they differ, yet you have no sooner passed the river Sind then the countries, the stones, the wandering tribes, manners and customs of the people are entirely those of Hindustan. After leaving Kashmir these hills contain many tribes and states, parganas and countries, and extend all the way to Bengal and to the shores of the great ocean. The countries and towns of Hindustan are extremely ugly. All its towns and lands have a uniform look. Its gardens have no walls. The great part of it is a level plain.

18. Hindustan is a country that has few pleasures to recommend it. The people are not handsome. They have no idea of the charm of the friendly society, of frankly mixing together, or of familiar intercourse. They have no genius, no comprehension of mind no politeness of manner, no kindness or fellow feeling, no ingenuity or mechanised invention in planning of executing their hand-craft work, no skill in design or architecture. They have no good horse, no good flesh, no grapes or muskmelon, no good fruits, no ice or cold water, no good food or bread in the bazar, no colleges, no baths, no candles, no torches and a candle stick. Hindustan is a large country and has abundance of gold and silver. The climate during rains is pleasant."

19. The great charm of Babur's memoir is in the character of Babur where we find after all the trials of a long life retaining the same kind affectionate heart and the same easy and social temper with which he set out in his career and in whom possession of power, grandeur had neither blunted the delicacy of his taste and diminished the sensibility to the enjoyment of nature and imagination. In this memoir we find emperor Babur a wonderful figure of humanity who never forgets parents, children, friends, about whom he has written in his memoir in most affectionate terms. Babur may be called a historian of his time. Babur records that Bengalis are famous in artillery.

20. Babur's poetic genius

Babur has recorded many instances of his display of poetic genius. Below is cited one:

One of Babur's chiefs Khwaja Kalan did not like the hot climate of Agra and repeatedly sought the permission of the emperor Babur who reluctantly accorded him permission to go to Kabul. Before he left he wrote the following couplet on the wall of his house :

> "If safe and sound I cross the Sind
> Blacken my face before I wish to Hind"

21. When Babur read this school boy humour, he considered it insolent of Khwaja Kalan to give such a parting message when he himself was to remain in India to look after the well-being of his subjects. Babur wrote on a piece of paper a reply in verse to Khwaja Kalan in these words:

> "Give a hundred thanks, Babur that the generous lord
>
> Has given you Sind and Hind and many a fort
>
> If you Khwaja be too weak for their heat
>
> Safely can you go to Kabul retreat."

22. Many stories about feats of physical courage are told about Babur. Only single story is related below:

A Rajput who was displeased with emperor Babur, resolved to murder him. For this purpose he bought a sharp knife and concealed it beneath his garments. The emperor used to wander alone on the street in plain cloth to see the condition of his subjects like Hazrat Abu Bakr and Omar. The Rajput was in wait to kill him when he was out for such unguarded wandering and he wandered about the street of Delhi to meet the emperor on the street. As the sun set, dusk fell the Rajput still was in his search. All on a sudden there was a great commotion. The street passengers shrieked and screamed and ran wildly in all directions and shop-keepers taking their children with them.

23.   The Rajput saw to his amazement that a mad elephant was out on the street, charging down the narrow street, its trunk beating the air in rage, its huge feet poundering on the ground. To his great horror the Rajput saw a small boy unware of the threatening danger stood on the way of the advancing mad elephant. A passerby cried out—"Save the child." Another shouted—"Who will endanger his life in saving an unknown boy."

24.   The elephant caught the boy with his trunk and was to trample him to death under its feet. Lo! a saviour appeared. Suddenly a tall man rushed forward and rescued the boy from the clutch of the elephant and took him unhurt in his arms.

25.   The child was frightened but was not hurt. The people shouted praise to this tall saviour of the boy. In his rush his turban fell away and he was recognised to be no other than the emperor Babur. This story testifies to the fearless spirit of Babur.

26.   The young Rajput saw this incident from a little distance. He was so much moved by the chivalry of Babur that all feelings of revenge melted away in him, and he felt at his feet. Babur asked—"What do you want, O young man?" The Rajput said—"I had an intention to kill you, but you have shown to me today it is better to save life than to take it." "Yes"—said the emperor,—"It is better to save than to destroy. You are a brave man, as you had the courage to say that you intended to kill me. You have spared my life. I shall make you my personal body guard to protect me at all times."

27.   Babur had stables and rest houses constructed at intervals on the road from Agra to Kabul. He introduced a mounted postal service. A band of horsemen carried letters and official documents between Agra and Kabul.

28.   Babur did not live long enough to reach a peaceful old age. He died in Agra in 1530 at 48 years of age. Great hardships of compaigns and heavy pressure of royal business much undermined his health. He was buried in the garden of Kabul.

29.   A story is told about his death. His beloved son Humayun fell seriously ill and his life was dispaired of Babur prayed to Allah to save his son's life and take his own life. Allah heard his prayer, and granted it. Babur thus showed an example of selfless sacrifice for others in his life.

30.   All the Mughul kings of Delhi were great lovers of learning and encouraged and helped education in all ways. Syed Muqaddar, minister and historian of Zahir-ud din Babur has written in history book that one of the functions of the public work department of Babur was to look after old colleges and schools and to build new ones.

XXXIX

HUMAYUN

1.   The emperor Babur had four sons, of whom Humayun was the eldest. His father Babur advised Humayun to treat his brothers with kindness and generosity when he ascended the throne. Humayun acted on his father's advise and gave his three brothers portions of his empire keeping Delhi for him.

2.   The soft hearted Humayun who is said to have trembled into life and tumbled out of it, was a poet, an astronomer and a mathematician. He had to wander about in a state of helplessness no doubt, but the intellectual grounding he received in his early years proved a comforting asset in his miserable life. The strain in which he has portrayed his feelings in the darkest hour of his life not only shows his ability to select the most suitable mode of expression but endorses his claim to poethood. Abdul Fazal and Fereshta have quoted profusely from Humayun's poetry. Humayun had a fine critical sense.

3.   Humayun was born at Kabul in the first week of Zilkad 913 A.H. On his father's death he was proclaimed emperor of India in 1530 A.C.

4.   In the history of the greater Mughuls the reign of Humayun has the appearance of an eclipse within a long period of bright sunshine. Humayun's reign was full of dangers and difficulties of all kinds.

5.   Humayun had fine fighting qualities. With his father's schooling and discipline behind him he was qualified for a career of conquest, but the task was not easy.

6.   When he assumed power, he found the empire in a state of

unstability and chaos. He was surrounded by enemies on the south and the east. His brother Kamran to whom he had given the Western Punjab and Kabul gave Humayun more troubles than all put together.

7.   The statements of the sequence of events in the first ten years of Humayun's rule (1530-40) were —"Humayun began with an attack on Jaunpur and he defeated Mahmud Lodi, brother of Ibrahim Lodi and put an end to Lodi rule in India."

8.   He next proceeded against Bahadur Shah, King of Gujrat and Malwa, and routed him in a decisive battle at Mandsur (1535) and took Mandsur and the fort of Champanir.

9.   Sher Khan, Afghan king of Bengal and Bihar threatence him from the east. He had to march against Sher Khan and he was successful and took Chunar and Gaur provinces of Bengal in 1538. Later a treaty of peace was signed between Humayun and Sher Khan by which Chunar was given back to Sher Khan.

10.   Humayun had to march for Agra and Sher Khan in violation of peace treaty made a night attack on Humayun at Chansa taking him unwares, defeating Humayun severely in 1539. A large number of Humayun's men were killed and drowned. Humayun had to fly for his life. While crossing the river Humayun lost his mount and had no means to cross the river.

11.   A water carrier under the name of Nizam seeing his flight and drowning state, lent him an inflated skin by which he crossed the river. In recognition of his signal service Humayun allowed him to sit for two hours as fully dressed as an emperor on the imperial throne with all the powers of the emperor.

12.   After Sher Khan's victory he declared himself as the emperor of India.

Humayun reached Agra. He took stock of his army which he found to be 90,000 fitted with proper equipment and prepared to avange the defeat of Chansa.

13. All this time his brother had been giving him trouble. His brother Askari had rebelled and was planning to depose him. Askari took Lahore and stayed there. When Humayun was arranging a final struggle with Sher Shah, Kamran was secretly negotiating with Sher Shah on his own account, but Sher Shah rejected his offer.

14. Humayun had to divert his attention owing to his brother's rebellion. When he reached Lahore he had Kamran in his power, but he, as soft hearted he was, excused him and did not put him to death as advised by his counsellors.

15. The final and decisive battle was fought between Humayun and Sher Shah near Kanauj in which Humayun sustained a crushing defeat (1540) and all hopes of conquest of Hindustan were now gone. Thus defeated by Sher Shah, betrayed by his brothers, deserted by most of his officers and men, Humayun stood alone and helpless in the God's world in the darkest moment of his life. Then he wandered through Marwar and Sind.

16. Humayun's marriage with Hamida Banu—mother of emperor Akbar, was little romantic. Humayun wanted to marry Hamida. She would not come. At last she said "To see kings one time is lawful, a second time is forbidden. I shall not come." At long last they were united in marriage.

17. The birth of Jalal-ud Din Akbar—this auspicious event took place, under menacing clouds of adversity at Umarkut on the night of full moon of Shaban 949 A.H. November 23, 1542.

18. At last despairing of all help and giving up all hopes, Humayun decided to seek asylum in Persia, and sent a letter to the Shah asking his permission to enter his kingdom. On receipt of this letter the Shah of Persia issued orders to all his officers to pay every attention in their power to Humayun, and to conduct themselves with respect to Humayun, and he sent letter to Humayun assuring his support and inviting him to his court.

19. Humayun stayed at Herat and other places inspecting places of interest, and ultimately reached Iran. At first some deputation waited on Humayun, then the princes came to welcome

him, and finally two kings met cordially embracing each other.
Shah offered him a hearty welcome.

20.   During Humayun's stay at Shah's court Humayun and
Shah were on most cordial terms and spent their time in hunting,
feasts and parties. Humayun gave Shah presents of a large diamond
and 250 rubies of Badakshan. He also gave a dinner party with
Indian dishes. Shah's sisters gave to Gulbadan a grand ladies
party, in which 1,000 ladies of high families attended.

21.   After staying for some time with the Shah Humayun bade
farewell. Shah helped him with 12,000 forces. The long period of
1545-54 was spent mostly in fighting round Kabul against Kamran.
In the battle of Kepchock (1550) Kamran was defeated.

22.   At last Humayun marched to India, marching from Kabul,
through Jalalabad, Peshwar he reached the Bank of Indus. Sultan
Sekander Sur with 80,000 men came to fight him and both Armies
camped opposite each other for a month, and ultimately both met
and Sekander Sur was defeated by superior strategy of Humayun,
and Afghan Army took to flight (June 1555). India once more lay
at Humayun's feet.

23.   But Humayun could not enjoy the fruit of his victory long.
Nor had he time to consolidate his conquest. One day Humayun
was on the roof of his library in Delhi palace where he with his
astronomers had been observing the transit of venus. When he was
descending the stairs, the call to prayer was sounded, and he, out
of respect, sat down on the steps. In the act of doing so, his foot
slipped and he fell, and died of injuries sustained on January 21,
1556.

24. Humayun's Character

The emperor Humayun was by disposition good-natured and
kind hearted, and of a benevolent and forgiving temperament.
Humayun showed uncommon tenderness in forgiving repeated
treachery of his brother Kamran. When the men of Bhakkar
brought Kamran to Humayun, he had not the heart to sign his
death-warrant, though Kamran behaved towards him in a perfidious

manner. Humayun always showed patience and forbearance. After a whole time spent in vile duplicity and shameless intrigine and treachery the climate was reached, when in course of fighting about Kabul, Kamran ordered his soliders to hold out the little Akbar against the firing of Humayun's army. Humayun had to give a cease-fire order to save his little son.

25. Humayun's officers were much dissatisfied but Humayun acted on the Quaranic saying—"Replace evil with something better."

26. Another incident shows how Humayun respected his stipulations and promises.

When Humayun besieged the fort of Chunar, its Garrision surrendered to Humayun on condition that their lives would be safeguarded, but Rumi Khan who was incharge of the artillery cut off the hands of 300 artillery men. When Humayun heard this, he was much shocked and grieved and exclaimed that it was wrong to violate the terms of treaty as the Quran commands—"Varily fulfil your promise, covenant do not transgress".

27. Humayun was greatly magnimous and noble in character. The following incident testifies to it:

Three men—namely Rushan Beg Kuka, Khwaja-Gazi Diwan and Sultan muhammad, who had been in Humayun's service deserted him and allied with Kamran. When Humayun was in Persia they poisoned the ears of the Shah against Humayun and advised him to imprison Humayun. Shah's sister and brother who were favourably disposed toward Humayun removed such poison and the Shah put all three into prison. Humayun knew all their plottings against him, but as he was noble and magnanimous Humayun prayed to the Shah for their forgiveness and release. The Shah was astonished at Humayun's magnanimity and nobility.

28. Humayun was a man of courage and resourcefulness like his father Babur, he never lost heart, even when sorely tried. In times of trials his self-reliance and self-confidence never foreshook him. He had an unshakeable faith in Allah and His help, and was always confident of his success.

29. Humayun's cast of mind was religious and scholarly. His father gave him good education. So when he grew upto his manhood he was a well-read and highly cultured person. He had a tendency for classical learning and was steeped in religious lore. He also inherited from his father a taste for art, poetry and music. He had a keen taste for painting. He made famous painter Mir Syed Ali to illustrate Dastani Amir Hamza on which Syed Ali and another famour painter Khwaja Abdus Samad worked. Humayun also took lesson in drawing.

It is said that when Humayun was sitting in a dressing gown at Umarkut a beautiful bird flew in his tent and he caught the bird and sent for painter and had a picture taken of the bird. This shows how fond he was of painting.

30. Humayun divided the total personnel of his countires and officers into three classes—namely (i) Ahle-Doulat, comprising emperor's relatives, nobles, ministers and the army; (ii) Ahle-Saadat, including Sadrs, Sayyids, learned and pious men, Gazis and poets; and (iii) Ahle-Murad, consisting of musicians, singers, and dancers. Various days of the week were allotted to these classess for their interview with the emperor. These three classess were further sub-divided into twelve tirs.

31. Among Humayun's buildings is Imarat-e-Tilsim (Talisman building) a set of three edifices. It had a cistern with a tunnel and surrounded by chamber and surmounted by a dome or vault (Qubba).

32. Humayun classified his administrative departments and offices according to four elements. His fire (sarkari atash) department covered arm, artillery, munition etc. His air department (sarkari hawai) included stables, kitchen ward robe and the like. His water department (sarkari aab) comprised sharbat khana, abdar khana, canals, navy, etc., and his earth department (sarkari khake) included buildings and agriculture.

33. Humayun's inventions

Humayun invented a new type of astrolebe called after his

name. Humayun was so fond of astronomy that he would never miss his lessons in this science even when he was on journey. He always had his teacher Shaikh Abul Qasim Jurjani by his side. His zeal for the subject was so great that during his exile wherever he went he keenly searched for new apparatus.

He studied mathematics for many years. In his march to India he brought a large number of books collected in Persia and Afghanistan. He set up a library on the top most storey of his "Shermandal", where he would go every afternoon to have discussion and debates with the learned scholars of his court. Humayun took keen interest in invention. He invented a floating garden which consisted of plants of wood in boats. He also invented a floating market consisting of boats. It was a boon to the people.

34. Humayun invented a moving palace made of wood, three storeys high. It was portable. It could be taken in pieces and reassembled. He also invented a moving bridge of boats over which an army could cross a river easily. He also invented a Kharga (tent) which was double-fold and was portable. It was a lofty tent surmounted by a ball or globe.

35. Humayun introduced another institution like the famous chain of justice which is associated with the name of emperor Jahangir. In place of chain, Humayun's was the drum of justice (table adl). It was placed close to the hall of audience. The rule was that in the case of an ordinary dispute the aggrieved party was to strike the drum once; where there was a demand for unpaid salary, it was struck twice; where property had been stolen, three times; and in case of murder, four times.

36. Though he was a great emperor, Humayun never considered himself above his fellow-men. He encouraged his people to lay their grievances before him for redress.

37. Humayun established a college at Delhi and turned a pleasant house into a grand library consisting of many thousand books.

X L

AKBAR THE GREAT

1. Abul Fath Jalal-al Din Muhammad, third Timurid emperor of Hindustan, was born at Umarkut in Sind on the 15th October 1542, was crowned at Kalanur in the Punjab on the 14th February 1556, and died in Agra on the 16th October 1605, leaving his throne to his son Salim (Jahangir).

2. Akbar traced his descent to Amir Timur Barlas (1336-1405), he was Babur's grandson and the sone of Humayun and Hameda Banu, a daughter of a Persian scholar in the service of Hindal, Babur's youngest surviving son.

3. Akbar was born in exile in one of the greatest centuries of history and in it he was the greatest ruler. Not Europe only was in mental ferment; it worked also in Hindustan, as indications of the presence of this intellectual wave. Kabir Panthi, the rawshanis, and the sufism of which Shaikh Mubarak Nagari was the exponent in closest touch with Akbar, appeared in India.

4. It is now a reliable fact that through his long life of intellectual activity Akbar did not master the arts of reading and writing. This is in him the more curious as he came of a family of traditional culture and as he lived not only amongst men of education but closely associated with him at least were two women accomplished in letters, his wife Salima Sultan, and his aunt Gulbadan.

5. Akbar's lack of instruction in childhood may well have been owing to his father's unsettled condition, but in adult life, only his own deliberate choice will explain it. A keen observer, avid of knowledge, a student of at least one branch of knowledge, religion, his dependence on the ear is a fact of great interest which falls into

place only when one recalls blind men who have been distinguished. It seems that Akbar learnt best by the living word.

6.   Akbar's long story of military success need not be related in details as it is known to every student of history. It will suffice to compare his territory at his accession and death. He had gone with his father to Hindustan in January, 1555 from Kabul and had been present at the decisive battle of Shirhind over Sekander Sur on the 22nd June, 1555 which gave Agra and Delhi to the Mughuls. When his father died (24th January, 1556) Akbar was with Bairam Khan Baharlu, pursuing Sekander in the Punjab. On that day the only land Akbar owned was a small part of the Punjab. Agra had been taken by Himu and Delhi had been evacuated by his general. Haram Begum and Sulaiman Badakhshani had seized Kabul.

7.   Akbar was then 14 years of age. When in 1605 Akbar laid aside the care of his empire, he left to his son Salim (Jahangir) a stable empire consisting of the whole of Upper India, Kabul, Kashmir, Bihar, Bengal, Orissa and a great part of the Deccan. This vast empire was acquired by Akbar the great by his grand military success in the course of his fifty year's reign.

8.   Great as he was as a soldier, it is as an administrator that he has gained the highest fame. His revenue reforms with which the Hindu Todarmall is closely associated, were effected in face of all opposition and pursued untiringly; so too was the safeguarding of the interest of the lowly people; Akbar had the genius of taking pains and the open-mindedness which is symbolised by his motto—"peace with all". By his liberal mindedness he ruled the majority Hindus and in return Hindus provided him with loyalty and faithful servants.

9.   Akbar made himself famous by his own pursuit of truth. It is a well-known fact that Akbar broke away from orthodox Islam and proclaimed an ecelectic Towhid "Illahi" or "Din-E-Illahi"—a divine faith of his own. This appears to be a pure theism, the common element of all the creeds he sought into. He allowed no priesthood and inculcated purity and plainness of living. But Touhid Illahi obtained outside his court practically no follower, and only eighteen names are recorded as those of the members of faith.

10. There are men to whose sufi influence Akbar's perversion from Islam was ascribed, Shaikh Mubarak Nagori and his sons. Akbar's earliest interest was with the sects within Islam itself and he became disgusted by the rancour of orthodox disputants, he married a Rajputani—the mother of Salim, and he studied Hinduism from priest and through Hindu scripture he had translated for him; sufi thinking was strong round him, and Persians were of his hom circle; he acquired a strong sympathy for the sun-worship of the Persis, a sympathy not likely to be less that Rajputs claim to be the children of the sun.

11. Nurul Hakk, a historian says—"The emperor Akbar tried to take the good from all the differing opinions and this with one sole object, the ascertaining of truth. What he finally accepted was but the basic fact of all creeds, man's first tenet and to this he added a plain rule of conduct."

12. Jalal-ud-Din Akbar is indeed a great study. The fact that so meagrely educated an emperor, coupled with military engagement, and success could have done so much to foster the arts and learning of his age still remains a riddle to be solved.

13. Akbar's wonderful common sense and the capacity to create around him an unexcelled intellectual atmosphere had led to a controversy about his education. Abul Fazul, a chief source of all information about Akbar calls him an "Ummi" (unlettered), but Abul Fazal himself admits that at the age of above 4 years Akbar's father entrusted Akbar to the care of Mullah Ussam-ud Din Ebrahim. Literate or unlettered Akbar had an admirable zeal for all kinds of intellectual pursuits. His fondness for books was so great that nearly all the outstanding books in Persian were read out to him. History, philosophy, religion, art, travel and topography: in short, books on all conceivable subjects were listened to, understood and digested by Akbar.

14. It was on the basis of his stock of information drawn from such source that he found himself able enough to take part in the religious and philosophical discussions of his "Ibadat Khana".

15. Akbar's common sense showed best when he heard the frivolous wrangles of the narrow-minded Mullas of his court, he

could see through the garb of sanctity worn by Makhdum-Ul Mulk, Sadar Jehan, and their tribe. Shaikh Mubarak and his sons had already cleared the way. They declared—"A just emperor has the right of ijtehad", and Akbar whose ambition knew no bound caught the idea and he found in it an opportunity to everlasting greatness and fame by founding his new faith Din-E Illahi.

16. Akbar like his father had a taste for poetry and some time composed verses himself. He was a great patron of learning. Tarekhi Alfi; Tarekhi Badauni Faizi's immense poetical work and treatise on music are a concrete proof of his great patronage.

17. Condition of Akbar's Empire

Khwaja Nizamuddin Ahmad Bakshi, author of the famous history "Tabakat-E-Akbari" best known as "Tarikhi Nizami" has given the following description of the Akbar's empire:

"Be not concealed that the country of Hindustan which is comprised within four climates and now included within the domain of Emperor Akbar Shah has its length from Hindukush on the border of Badakshan to the country of Orissa which is on the border of Bengal, from west to east is 1680 legal kos. The soil is well-adapted for cultivation and within each kos are several inhabited villages. At present the time namely A.H. 1002 Hindustan contains 3,200 towns and upon each there are dependent 200, 300, 1,000 and 1,500 villages. The wholes Hindustan yields a revenue of 640 crores; of the town 120 are large cities."

18. The divisions of Akbar's empire according to Muhammad Hanafi, the author of the history book "Majlis-Us Salatin". The whole of Hindustan during the rule of Akbar was divided into fourteen subas or provinces; namely Delhi, Agra, Punjab, the Province of Kabul, the Province of Dakhin or Ahmad Nagar, the Province of Khandesh and Berar, the Province of Malwa, the Province of Gujrat, the Province of Bihar including Patna, the Province of Oudh with Dependencies, the Province of Ajmir, the Province of Allahabad, the Province of Sind including Multan, Thatta and Dhakkor, and the Province of Bengal which was equal to three kingdoms.

19. A fuller description of the conditions of India during the time of the first six great Mughul emperors including Akbar has been given thus:

"India is a large country and it is so extensive that other countries are not equal to it. It is populated in all places. It abounds on all quarters and in every district with cities, towns and villages, caravans, sarais, forts, citadels, mosques, temples, monasteries, cells, magnificent buildings, delightful gardens, fine trees, pleasant green fields, running streams, and tempestuous rivers, on all the public roads and streets strong bridges are made over every river and rill and embankments are also raised, lofty minerats are made at the distance of each kos to indicate the road and at every two parasang inns are built of strong masonry for travellers to dwell in and take rest. At each inn can be had every kind of food and drink, all sorts of medicines, all sorts of necessary instruments, and utensils. On all roads shadowy and fruitful trees are planted on both sides. Wells and tanks are dug which contain fresh and sweet water in abundance. The passengers go along the roads under the shadow of trees amusing themselves, eating the fruits, drinking cold water. The merchants, tradesmen and all travellers without any fear of thieves and robbers take their goods and loads safe to their destination. The whole of the country is very fertile. There are mines of diamonds, rubies, gold, silver, copper lead, and iron. The soil is generally good. All kinds of food grains are in abundance."

20. As Akbar was a minor, at the time of his father's death Bairam Khan was elected to act as his agent during his minority. Bairam Khan was a famous soldier and a good writer. Bairam entered the service of Humayun and served him faithfully and with devotion.

21. Akbar was brought up in the mountainous country of Afghanistan. He led a free life in a free country and developed a strong physique and habit of hard working. The young prince became an excellent horseman and a sure shot. He was a good sportsman, a good swimmer and a good runner.

22. Akbar on reaching majority ascended the throne of Delhi at the age of eighteen and mightily ruled for fifty years. Akbar was

a great general and an excellent army leader popular with his armies who could create confidence in them and could inspire them to great enterprises. His soldiers respected him as a leader and loved him as a comrade who could fight with them bravely.

23. Akbar was a great statesman. He was the first to follow a policy to unite Hindus and Muslims of India for common good of the people and he treated Hindus equally and tried to make them consider themselves as the equal citizens of the Mughul empire and not to think themselves as a conquered people.

24. Like Sher Shah Suri Akbar was the first Mughul emperor of India who dreamt a dream of an United India. But in spite of his very just policy and equal treatment to the Hindus, there were some Hindu princes who did not submit to Akbar and Akbar had to wage war againt these Hindu Rajas and in all his wars with the Hindu Rajas he was successful. Gradually the Rajputs submitted to his sovereignty. Man Singha and others became his faithful supporters.

25. Akbar declared— "He was servant of all and master of none." This spirit of humility, the policy of tolerance, as enjoined by Islam to non-Muslims, equal treatment to all his subjects, and his policy fair field and no favour, won the day and became for the first time the ruler of an United India never conceived before.

26. Akbar was against any sort of oppression and injustice. When the Governor of Malwa ruled like a tyrant over the people, he undertook a very arduous journey to Malwa and punished the corrupt governor after hot pursuit.

27. Akbar like his father followed the Quranic injunction to return evil with good, with something better. During his reign the Portugese pirates appeared in the Indian Ocean and began to hunt their piracy on the sea. The Portugese pirates heavily armed used to burn or sink the ships. Once a Portugese desecrated the holy quran. Akbar's mother Hamida hinted similar treatment to the Bible. But Akbar said : "Bible is also respected by a Muslim. It will be evil for evil if I similarly treat the holy Bible."

28. Akbar did not like a life of ease and luxury, and lived a simple life avoiding pomp and grandeur. He was a good huntsman, and liked sports. At that time the city of Lahore had dense jungles where there were many lions; and lions came out at nights and killed the cattle of villagers who lived in the outskirts of the city and even the villagers who happened out door were killed by the lions.

29. Once Emperor Akbar arranged a large hunting party to kill as many lions as possible. Akbar rode on an elephant into the forest at the head of the party. His valiant noble Musaheb Khan was with him. All on a sudden three huge lions sprang out from dense jungles and charged the royal elephant. One lion sprang up so high in the air that it's claws caught in the clothes of the emperor. The furious lion opened out it's mouth to bite, but Musaheb Khan at once rushed to the rescue and caught the lion by it's mains and speared it.

30. Akber died after he had reigned for half a century. He is considered as one of the greatest enlightened ruler of the world. In that dark age of intolerance, oppression, serfdom, injustice, discord and dissension he held out the torch of unity, equal justice, equal treatment to all and lighted the torch of broad tolerance and respect to all religions.

31. The story goes that when Akbar was born at Umarkut, his father Humayun had nothing to give to his nobles and soldiers as present on this occasion according to time honoured custom, he brought out a musk and held it upto them and said— "May Allah spread the name and fame of my infant son as the smell of this musk". Allah heard his prayer, it is said, his sons's name and fame still adorns the pages of human history.

32. Akbar established many schools and colleges where Hindu and Muslim students received the same instruction. Blockmann, an European scholar who visited Delhi during Akbar's reign found a great college founded by Akbar at Fatehpur Sikri like of which few travellers can name. Akbar also set up a large library, of rare books and appointed a full-time librarian, Mullah Pir Muhammad for this library.

33. Several other many schools and colleges were founded by Akbar, at Agra, Delhi, Ahmadabad and in many other cities where students of all nationalities could go for a higher education. These colleges were mostly residential and liberal monetary help was given by the government for their maintenance. Besides government educational institutions, many private schools and colleges were founded and maintained by nobles and grandees of the imperial court at Delhi and at other places, and colleges such as Mir Ali Beg's academy at Agra. In 1961 Akbar's nurse Muham Tuga founded a college at Delhi.

XLI

JEHANGIR

1. The Emperor Akbar was succeeded by his son Salim, known as Emperor Jehangir in 1605 A.C. Jehangir is called the aesthete. He was indeed the foremost poet in his family. His early education had been quite liberal and intensive and he had fully imbibed the unorthodox spirit of his father's court. Religious wranglings and prosaic politics could hardly attract his romantic mind. He always looked at things with artist's eyes from an aesthetic point of view. His own memoir and captivating personality of Emperor Jehangir. Its simplicity, persecuity, beautiful diction, facile charming expression and command of the subject matter are special features that reveal the inner light and wealth of its royal author Jehangir Badshah. His picturesque wordings, pen pictures and vivid descriptions and expressions are so life like that one cannot but be charmed and astonished at its depth of vision and acute keenness of observation. Read his delineation and picturing of dainty flowers and beautiful birds and you will feel that you are in the midst of them. But the delicacy, flourish, comprehensiveness and vividness of his genius is best manifested and displayed in his poetry and painting.

2. The most outstanding feature of th character of this creative artist and aesthete was that Jahangir Hada remarkable sense of judgement so that whenever he discusses any poem he seems to reveal in its minutest details and the minutest shades of meanings and the most tender films of emotion. Allama Shibli says— "Jehangir's taste for poetry was as sound as that of only great critic. Whatever he has said about any poet, it is the last word in criticism." His choice of selection from poems of poets Urfi, Naziri and Abu Talib Kalim demonstrate his exquisite taste. The art of painting engaged more of Jehangir's time and talents. Shaikh Abul Hoque's Tajkeratul Aulia and Mir Uzad Dowla's Farhang Jahangiri are the best and most learned and scholarly works of his time.

3. Jehangir proved to be a benevolent and kind hearted monarch and showed and exhibited the same qualities of justice and compassion during his rule as father Akbar had displayed before him.

4. Jehangir is accused in history that he caused the death of Nurjahan's husband Sher Afghan in order to marry his widow Nurjahan, but Ikbalnama Jahangiri written by Muhammad Hadi falsify this allegation against Jehangir. This history has been written by Muhammad Hadi who held a high post in Jehangir's court and knew every details of his life. This history is also known as Jahangirnama.

This most authentic history of Jehangir's reign records the incident leading to the death of Sher Afghan, husband of Nurjahan. It records: "When Jehangir ascended the throne he appointed Sher Afghan governor of Burdwan and Kutubuddin was sent to watch his activities. Kutubuddin reported against Sher Afghan's mischievous activities and the emperor directed him to send Sher Afghan to the Imperial Court. Kutubuddin called at Sher Afghan and met him alone. Sher Afghan suspected a foul design and stabbed Kutubuddin in the belly, and Kutubuddin cried out and his attendants killed Sher Afghan. Nurjahan after Sher Afghan's death was sent to Delhi and Emperor Jehangir who was greatly distressed at the murder of Kutubuddin entrusted her to the care of his royal mother. Nurjahan remained with her mother unnoticed for sometime. In the sixth year of his reign and on the occasion of the celebration of the Nauruz (New Year's Day) Emperor Jehangir happened to see her, fell in love and married her."

5. The historian then remarks— "It is impossible to describe the beauty and wisdom of Nurjahan. Many matters which were presented to her when a difficulty arose she immediately solved it. Whoever threw himself upon her protection. She saved him from tyranny and oppression. If ever she learnt that any orphan girl was destitude and friendless, she would bring about her marriage."

This historian's version disproves the general story that Jehangir before he became an emperor fell in love with Nurjahan and wanted to marry her but Emperor Akbar got her married to Sher Afghan and sent him to Bengal.

6.   The Queen Empress Nurjahan was a lady or matchless beauty and of great intelligence. Not only was she externally beautiful, she was also internally illuminated. She was given excellent and sound education. She was a poet of no mean calibre. She could hold her well in battle of wits. Jehangir frequently competed with her in verse. Jehangir would recite a few lines of a poem, Nurjahan promptly would come up with an apt reply.

7.   Nurjahan played active role in the administration of the vast empire of Jehangir. It is said that the Emperor Jehangir was a king in name only, and the Queen Nurjahan in reality ruled the empire with justice and benevolence. Jehangir left every decision to her, so sagacious and judicious and wise she was. She was a great lover of justice and hated mis-use of power and oppression.

8.   The Queen Nurjahan not only excelled in virtues of head and heart, she was also expert in physical feats, such as shooting, chugan. The Mughul emperors were very fond of hunting wild beasts in jungles. Nurjahan was also so. The Queen Nurjahan often accompanied her husband in his hunting expeditions.

9.   Once it so happened that tigers from dense jungles were terrorising the villagers and a complaint was made to Jehangir. Jehangir ordered a hunting expedition to be arranged. Nobles and huntsmen gathered with their guns and spears. Jehangir with his Queen Nurjahan started on the hunting expedition to kill the tigers. The hunting party penetrated dense forests. The beaters cried out— "tiger, tiger". Nurjahan sought the permission of her husband to shoot first of all. All on a sudden four fierce tigers sprang up and their furious roarings, echoing and reachoing in deep forests created a hell. Even the royal elephant was alarmed and began to move to and fro. The mahoots tried to keep the royal elephants to stand still but could not do so. They remained restless. Four tigers leapt up towards royal howda, and every body held up his gun to shoot, but as the queen was the first to shoot, none shot.

10.   The brave Queen Nurjahan, disregarding rolling motion of her elephant shot at first two big tigers and she killed the remaining two. She was rewarded by the emperor for her extra ordinary daring feats.

11.   Jehangir ruled the empire from 1605 to 1622 and proved a just ruler and a great reformer.

12.   The Wakiati Jahangiri which is the authentic autobiography and history of Jehangir's reign written by Jehangir himself contains some interesting facts about his reign. Below is reproduced in brief some of the facts:

13.   The Chain of Justice

"The first order which I (Jehangir) issued was for the sitting up of a "chain of justice", so that if the officers of the courts of justice should fail in the investigation of the complaints of the oppressed and in granting them redress the injured persons might come to this chain and shake it and so give notice of wrongs done to them. I ordered that chain should be made of pure gold thirty gauze in length with sixty bells upon it. Its weight was four maunds. The one end of this chain was firmly attached to a battlement of the fort of Agra, and the other end to a stone column in the bank of river."

14.   Twelve Institutes of Jehangir

I established 12 ordinances to be observed and to be the common rule of practice throughout my dominion:—

(i)   *Prohibition of illegal Cesses*— "I forbade the levies of duties under the names of tangha mir bahari together with the taxes of all descriptions which the Jaigirdars of every Suba and Sarkar had been in the habit of exacting for their own benefit."

(ii)   *Regulation about highway Robbery and Theft*— "On those roads which were the scenes of robbery and theft and in those portions of roads which were far away from habitations, the Jaigirdars of the neighbourhood were ordered to build a sarai or mosque and to sink a well so as to be the means of cultivation and to induce people to settle there. If these place were khalisa, the government officials were to carry out these provisions."

(iii)   *Free Inheritance of the Properties of the Deceased*—

"No one was to open the package of merchants on the roads without their consent. When a person died on the roads, his properties were to be allowed to his descendants by inheritance without any interference from any one. When no heir left, then officers were appointed to take charge of the properties and to spend them according to Law of Islam in building mosques, sarais, repairing of broken bridges, and digging of tanks and wells."

(iv) *Wine and all kinds of Intoxicating Liquors forbidden*— "Wine and every sort of intoxicating liquor is forbidden, msut neither be made nor sold."

(v) *Prohibitions of taking forcible possession of house and cutting of the noses and ears of criminals*— "No one was to take up his abode in the dwelling of another. I made an order prohibiting every one from cutting the noses and ears of criminals for any offence and I made a vow to heaven that I would never inflict such punishment."

(vi) *Prohibition of Gazbi*— "The officers of khash land and the Jaigirdars are not to take the lands of the rayats by force and they also not to form conexions without permission."

(vii) *Building of Hospitals and Appointments of Physicians to attend the sick*— "Hospitals were to be built in large cities and doctors were to be appointed to attend the sick. The expenses were to be borne from the royal treasury."

(viii) His 8th ordinance prohibits the slaughter of animals on certain days.

His 9th, 10th, and 11th ordinances relate to general confirmation of Mansabs, Jagir and Aima land; and 12th ordinance relates amnesty to prisoners.

New names for Coins— "Gold and silver coins of various weights were made and to each one of which I gave distinct name. The coins of 100 tolas I called Nure-Shahi; the 50 tolas Nure-Sultani; the 20 tolas Nure-Doulat; 10 tolas Nure-karam; 5 tolas Nure-Mehr; 1 tola Nure-Jhani; ½ tola Nurani; 1¼ tola Rawjai.

Silver Coins— "I called the 100 tolas kanka Bitali; the 50 tolas Kanka Bibakht; 5 tolas Kanka Fisad; 1 tola Jahangiri; ½ tola Sultani; the 1¼ tola Arshari; and the 110/1 tola Khair Kabul."

Jehangir also records that he remitted many crores of rupees of transit duties.

Wars in Bengal—Under this heading Jehangir writes— "Just at this time a despatch arrived from Islam Khan with the intelligence of the defeat of the enemy, and the deliverance of the country of Bengal from the Sway of Uthman the Afghan. Bengal is an extensive country situated in the second clime. Its length is 450 cos extending from Bandar Chatgam (The port of Chittagong) to Gahri and its breadth from the northern mountain and to the province Maduran (Midnapore) is 220 kos. Its revenue amounted to sixty crores of Dinnars. In former its governors always maintained one lakh of foot soldiers 1,000 elephants and 400 to 500 war boats.

From the time of Sher Khan Afghan and his son Salim Khan, this country remained in the possession of Afghans. At last my father conquered from Daud Kirani, the ruler of this land. From that time the country had been governed by the servants of the empire. Mansingh was the governor of Bengal for long. I recalled him and appointed Kutubuddin to succeed him but he was assassinated. So I sent Jehangir Kuli Khan to succeed him, but he soon died. So I appointed Islam Khan to be the governor of Bengal. Islam Khan took and subdued all refractory elements and brought peace and order in the country.

15. Jehangir died in 1622 A.C. while he was on a visit to Rajauri in Kashmir and was buried in Lahore according to his expressed desire. He was buried at Shahadara near the river Ravi. Nurjahan and Jehangir's son built a most beautiful mausoleum over his tomb. After the death of Jehangir Nurjahan lived a secluded life and she erected a small tomb near her husband's mausoleum as she desired to be buried near her husband after her death.

Jehangir's mausoleum at Shahadara still remains a monument of great beauty, grandeur and of historical interest. The garden and beautiful groves of plants and trees surrounding it present a charming scenery and sober and serene setting for this magnificent Mughul architecture.

16. Emperor Jehangir left for us a unique legacy of his own — namely his autobiography written by himself. It is a plain record of all events that Jehangir thought worthy of record. This work is very interesting and shows Jehangir in true character. In it Jehangir has recorded frankly all his weakness, even he has confessed his faults with candour; and an unbiassed perusal of his autobiography leaves a favourable impression as to Jehangir's character and his talents on the minds of the readers.

17. Like his father Jehangir was fond of jewels. He was a mighty hunter and took pleasure in sports even upto the later years of his life. He was a lover of nature, both animate and inanimate and viewed nature with a shrewd and keen observer's eyes. In his memoirs he mentions the peculiarities of many animals and birds. He was also a minute observer of plants, trees, flowers, fruits etc. and took keen interests in their developments and bestowed thought and time upon them.

18. Jehangir's autobiography comprises about 823 pages and is preserved in the Royal Asiatic Society. There are two autobiographies—one is bigger than the other and the bigger is proved to be his memoir written by him.

19. Jehangir as an emperor of India acquired name and fame as a mighty ruler, and many great foreign countries sent ambassadors to his court. Shah Abbas, the Shah of Persia sent to Emperor Jehangir an ambassador with valuable presents and Jehangir sent his reply to the Persian Shah in which he included couplets composed by him.

20. During Jehangir's reign European traders began their trading in India. The Portuguese was already in the field. The East India Company of the United Kingdom sent a delegation under Thomas Roe to conclude trade treaty with the Emperor Jehangir. Roe reached the Mughul court which was then at Ajmir in December 1915 and for nearly three years he followed in the train of the

emperor, striving deligently to carry out the object of his mission; but he found that the conclusion of any commercial treaty with the emperor was not possible as the Jehangir's advisers opposed such treaty on the ground that such treaty would extend the struggle between two European nations and that would be extended to other parts of India as the Portuguese were opposing the entry of the English in the field of Indian trade. Roe left India in 1619 but before his departure he was able to establish regular English factories at Surat, Agra, Ahmedabad and Broach.

21.   Emperor Jehangir sometimes wore simple dress and travelled in disguise unaccompanied by any one at night along the street to see the condition of his subjects and to redress their grievances. It so happened that while in his nocturnal journey dressed as a workman, the emperor entered an inn used by craftsmen. The craftsmen present welcomed him. Jehangir relished much the talk and laughter of a man who sat near him. The emperor asked for the best meal available in the inn and invited the craftsmen present to eat with him. After the meal, the emperor asked the name of the man who sat near him. The man was taken aback and replied— "It is strange, you don't know me. Everyone knows me in this city. I am the Sekander the weaver." The emperor said— "My dear Sekander, I invite you to my palace to dine with me tomorrow night."

22.   Jehangir had innate sense of humour and wit, and he could cut a joke with any one. The next night Jehangir came out on his elephant with stately bodyguard to search out the home of the weaver whom he met in the inn last night. The royal procession found Sekander outside his humble hut—weaving cloth laboriously on his loom. He was gazing awide at the royal cavalcade approaching him. At this a member of the royal cavalcade came running to Sekander and shouted— "Where is the Sekander the weaver," Sekander taken aback enquired— "Why do you want Sekander." "Because the emperor has invited him to dine with him"—answered the man. Sekander now remembered his foolish boasting in the previous night. In the mean time the emperor drew closer to Sekander. His royal servant thundered— "where is Sekander tell me atonce. Are you deaf ? Why do you not reply?" Now Sekander

remembered the last night's happenings in the inn. He retorted to the royal servant— "If your emperor is so dull as to take vain boasting as truth, then he is a great fool as I am." The Emperor Jehangir heard his remark but was not enraged. On the contrary he rewarded the weaver for his outspokenness.

23. There are other fine stories about Jehangir's noble-ness ang greatness. Some may be interesting and may be narrated.

Once the Emperor Jehangir was riding on a royal elephant on the streets, and a huge crowd was watching him. All on a sudden a man from the crowd cried out with great laughter— "O, I will be glad to purchase this royal elephant at rupees ten tankas." The emperor heard him and ordered his arrest. The following day when he was produced before the emperor, he asked him— "Do you still want to purchase my elephant?" "No, Your Majesty, the man who wanted to purchase is not here. I am only his agent", said the man.

24. Jehangir was not angry with his evasive reply but appreciated his presence of mind and rewarded him with an elephant.

25. Jehangir's Character and Constructive works:

Jehangir was very eager to encourage and help trade and commerce, and tourist trade and travel, and for this purpose he made the great high way from Agra to Lahore safe and comfortable for all such persons. He issued instructions to all the zamindars to plant trees at halting places and he also had sarais, inns, mosques, built at every 8 kos along the Agra-Lahore road for the convenience and comforts of travellers. Each rest house provided shelter to traders, travellers and pilgrims, and it also provided meals and pure drinking water. A permanent staff was attached to each rest house to look after it and cater to the needs of travellers. Being encouraged by the emperor many Zaigirdars and noblemen laid out gardens of flowers and orchards of fruits along this highway, and vegetables and fruits were supplied to these rest houses.

26. Like his ancestors, Emperor Jehangir was a just king. He did not like oppression and punished the oppressors with iron hand.

Syed Khan was his commander of his Lahore army. When the emperor heard that there were some in his army who had oppressed the people, he sent his order to his commander Syed Khan— "All my subjects, high and low, are equal in Islam, and also in my eyes. I never tolerate any oppression or injustice by any of your men. If any of your men had committed any wrong or injustice, punish him or them severely." Syed Khan replied— "Yes, Your Majesty, I will do my utmost to punish any man in my army if I find him doing any oppression on any other man."

27.   Jehangir was a great builder. He erected many fine buildings at Agra, Delhi and Lahore, and laid out many beautiful gardens at these places. He built very fine bridges over rivers and canals. Many of his architectural monuments survive to this day through ravages and vecissitudes of time.

28.   Akbar's son Jehangir, as the author of the Tarikhi Jame Jahan, was a great lover of learning. He repaired all schools, madrassahs and colleges, even including those which had been abandoned as long as thirty years ago, filled them with students and professors, and liberally helped them with money.

◆◆◆◆

THE LIFE OF SALADIN (1137-1193 A.D)
Beha-Ed-Din

The author accompained the Sultan on many important compaigns and watched him at close quarters. So this is the most authentic history on the life of Sultan Salah-ud- Din Aiyyoobi.

Demy 8vo   **pp XX + 420**   **2nd Edn. 1992 Rs. 250/-**

THE POLITICAL THOUGHT OF IBN TAYMIYAH
Prof. Qamaruddin Khan

This book is perhaps the first attempt to presenting a systematic and objective study of the political philosophy of Ibn Taymiyah (661-728/1263-1328) one of the greatest original thinkers who wrote on the political philosophy of Islam.

Demy8vo   **pp X + 219**   **2nd Edn. 1992   Rs.125/-**

THE ROAD TO MAKKAH
M. Asad

Muhammad Asad tells the story of his road of discovery, his journeys through Muslim countries, and the gradual changes in his way of thinking which were to bring him, inevitably as it seemed, to Islam. The road is a road of adventure, of continuous revelation; travels in Palestine, Trans Jordan, Arabia, North Africa, Turkey, Persia; friendship with the Bedouins of the desert, and with kings such as Ibn Saud of Arabia and Reza Shah of Iran. As he penetrated to the hearts of these countries he came to understand the rational principles of Islam, and to know the troubled history and politics of the Muslims.

The Road to Makkah describes the happines and sense of reality brought to one man by the Muslim way of life.

Demy 8vo   **pp XIII + 382**   **1992**   **H. B. Rs. 125/-**
                                              P. B. Rs. 80/-